PHILANTHROPY'S ROLE IN CIVILIZATION

PHILANTHROPY'S ROLE IN CIVILIZATION

Its Contribution to Human Freedom

BY Arnaud C. Marts

PRESIDENT, MARTS AND LUNDY, INC.

Foreword by Dr. Karl T. Compton

HARPER & BROTHERS, PUBLISHERS, NEW YORK

These Americans are the most peculiar people in the world. You'll not believe it when I tell you how they behave. In a local community in their country a citizen may conceive of some need which is not being met. What does he do? He goes across the street and discusses it with his neighbor. Then what happens? A committee comes into existence and then the committee begins functioning on behalf of that need, and you won't believe this but it's true. All of this is done without reference to any bureaucrat. All of this is done by the private citizens on their own initiative.

Americans of all ages, all conditions, and all dispositions consistently form associations . . . to give entertainments, to found seminaries, to build inns, to construct churches, to diffuse books, to send missionaries to the antipodes. . . .

The health of a democratic society may be measured by the quality of functions performed by private citizens.

ALEXIS DE TOCQUEVILLE,
on the occasion of his
visit to America in 1830

Contents

Foreword

by Dr. Karl T. Compton

CHAIRMAN OF THE CORPORATION AND
FORMER PRESIDENT, MASSACHUSETTS INSTITUTE OF TECHNOLOGY

I JOIN the thirty million Americans who contribute to good causes in welcoming the publication of this volume which undertakes to interpret to our citizens and to the rest of the free world the vast significance of American freedom to create and maintain such agencies as we ourselves may desire for the education, health, and betterment of our communities.

The story of these voluntary enterprises is the story of America at its best. Our freedom to give to such institutions or not to give—in our own way and for our own reasons—is one of the significant manifestations of the American Way of Life. This is an appropriate time to give fresh consideration to the enormous contribution which voluntary philanthropy has made to our national and international well-being.

Recently I had occasion, when speaking before a gathering of distinguished chemical engineers, scientists, and industrialists, to say:

Our national prosperity has been based on the environment which we often describe, in an inclusive way, as the American System of Free Enterprise. When we compare its success to that of such competing systems as Socialism or the Authoritarian State, we have practical proof of its value. We ascribe its success to the scope which it gives to the ambition and enterprise of free individuals. . . . Ability, ambition, an element of luck—all subject to competitive factors—are the bases of careers, as distinguished from traditions or regulations. This is the ideal. We should be alert to preserve it.

Obviously, in such a complex society as ours, some regulations and safeguards are necessary in the over-all interest. The public must be protected against exploitation by selfish groups. . . . All must share equitably in supporting the public services of government and national defense. These things are obvious and universally accepted.

But there are insidious dangers lest these necessary functions of government be extended in directions which are not in the public interest and which threaten our free enterprise system. . . .

While the context of this statement referred to technological achievement, it is equally important in the field of our educational, social, and cultural services. On the one hand, we should be keenly aware of the proper role of voluntary philanthropy— on the other, of the proper role of governmental subsidy and responsibility.

Freedom in America is indivisible. We cannot be free in one aspect of our life, and controlled in another, without danger to our total free society. It is essential that we have a clear-cut understanding of the values and bases of freedom in our cultural enterprises as well as in the fields of politics and business. This volume, therefore, is a needed and useful guide to our understanding of voluntary philanthropy as an important element in the American Way of Life.

Dr. Marts's long association with thousands of men and women across the nation in their voluntary services and gifts to our private philanthropic institutions has provided him with the experience with which to appraise and describe philanthropy's role in civilization. I have had the privilege of seeing Dr. Marts in action and of appreciating his technique and philosophy. He deserves the thanks of thoughtful people for providing this addition to our meager literature on this vital phase of American culture.

Introduction

THIS book tries to gather together the experiences of more than thirty years in the field of organization and fund raising for a wide range of independent agencies. If it seems to glorify philanthropy, that is what it has set out to do—for I doubt whether it is possible to overestimate its creative role in the development of western civilization.

It has seemed to be an appropriate time to discuss the subject because of greatly increased governmental participation, during the last two decades, in many forms of welfare and education. To many, these changes appear to be "trends" and "inevitable." They accept the doctrine that there is only one way for the pendulum to swing. They have momentarily lost sight of the large part that philanthropy is still playing in those countries where freedom lives. We shall try to paint that view into the vast and complex picture of our national life. To provide the basis for a vital, balanced life in a modern society both poles are equally necessary—laws and freedom, taxation and voluntary giving.

The backbone of modern social structure is our body of civil laws. We have created for ourselves an elaborate framework of regulations which prescribe our public conduct, collect taxes for the support of the institutions the laws have founded, and provide the penalties, police, and courts to coerce those reluctant to observe the laws. Thus, much of our life becomes involuntary.

Law, however, falls short of defining the limits of personal life in America. While we depend upon it to give stability to our society, we make use of countless spontaneous undertakings to give life fullness, character, and meaning. It is of these voluntary efforts which this book speaks, of the overflow of mankind's instinctive longing for improvement, of his ardent efforts—far beyond the law's *thou shalt*—to minister to the well-being and culture of his fellows.

There are at least 500,000 organized units of such voluntary endeavor in America. There are no less than thirty million persons of social sensitiveness who give energy and money to one or more such organizations. An astonishing amount of our cultural and spiritual advance has been achieved by these self-directed agencies. Men and women thus give their efforts and their resources, not because they can ever be repaid financially, but because such efforts make life richer, more kindly, and more noble.

The total annual volume of taxation for the support of all compulsory public functions and institutions is approximately eighty-six billions of dollars. These compulsory assessments we cannot avoid; they are onerous—the object of instinctive and mounting complaint. But, complain as we do over taxation, we then proceed cheerfully enough, and without the slightest compulsion, to give an additional four and a half billions voluntarily to other social agencies which we have created.

What and where are these 500,000 voluntary agencies? What techniques are used to induce the American people to build and maintain them with freely given annual gifts of well over four billion dollars? This book endeavors to describe, explain, and appraise some of the major enterprises, and the manner of their support. Historians have been curiously silent in regard to these unofficial benevolent activities which have taken the lead in the development of so many important phases of our national culture.

If a history of the American people were ever written from a human, personal point of view, it would tell a new story. It would largely be given over to a study of how we have used our political freedom to found and maintain our great network of private agencies—instrumentalities of education, health, religion, culture, reform, character building, social welfare, and humanitarian aspiration. But our histories are written by students of politics, of government, of militarism, of economics, of commerce. Little is said about the generous efforts of private citizens to establish voluntary institutions for the service of their fellows.

Yet these self-directed private citizens—acting of their own free will—have been the real artificers of our Republic. The self-sustaining agencies which they have created have been constantly pumping into the body politic transfusions of the vital lifeblood of morality—true liberalism and enlightened humanitarianism—without which the body would inevitably deteriorate.

It has been my privilege to work closely with thousands of men and women across the nation in behalf of most types of voluntary activity mentioned in this book. I have seen them give energy when they were weary and needed rest; I have seen them give time when their own affairs urgently called; I have seen them give money when they were obliged to let their own wants go unsatisfied; and I have seen them made happier because of these voluntary choices and efforts. In this portrayal of philanthropy I have attempted to reflect something of the mind and spirit which animates these "lovers of mankind" who derive deep satisfactions from their unselfish service to their fellow men.

"Love thy neighbor as thyself" is no modern concept. It is as old as the oldest ethical religions. Wherever men have lived under that warm-hearted impulse they have created—without any suggestion from rulers, lords, governors, or selectmen—voluntary agencies to serve their communities.

Our American society is so rich, so resourceful, so complicated that it could never have been planned from above, by any central authority. It was conceived and brought into being in the hearts, the minds, and the free wills of the people themselves.

For ideas and materials that have helped to round out this book, the author wants to pay acknowledgment to many persons—a number of whom are mentioned in the text. In the nature of voluntary philanthropy, as a co-operative process, this is necessarily so. The most valuable lessons have come out of these close associations with leaders and workers in projects, large and small, too numerous to mention.

I wish to record my special thanks to Mr. F. Emerson Andrews, director of philanthropic research of Russell Sage Foundation, for his careful reading of the galley proofs and for his helpful criticisms and suggestions.

For various expressions of the philanthropic impulse I am indebted to more people and sources than could be mentioned by name. For years I have been jotting these down, sometimes losing track of the exact original source. Many of these expressions—

found in newspaper stories, speeches, or reports—said the things I have been trying to say for thirty years, but said them better. I beg the indulgence of the authors if I have sometimes failed to acknowledge the exact source, and thank them for their unconscious help in presenting a great American idea which so many of us hold in common.

It is with particular appreciation, however, that mention is made of two colleagues in the fund-raising profession who have made specific contributions to this volume. Louis W. Robey contributed, out of his rich experience, the paragraphs in Chapter XI on fund raising as a profession—a remarkably fine statement of ideals (pages 170-172). George E. Lundy—one of the ablest men this profession has produced—who is well acquainted with the problems of fund raising in wartime as well as throughout the past three decades, has contributed comments which shed surprising light on that subject.

These chapters have been written over a period of eighteen years, out of a desire to put into definite form certain leading factors bearing on our theme. In a rough sense, they are planks in the platform and program of American philanthropy. They have been edited, supplemented, and woven into book form by a long-time friend, Ernest B. Chamberlain—author of *Our Independent Schools*—who has had wide experience in education and in other fields of philanthropy.

The seven sections into which the book is divided present the chief questions one encounters in trying to cover this many-sided subject. But this is not a book on methods; several books have been published on "How to Raise Money."

To those of us who have spent most of our professional lives in its service, American philanthropy is a tangible and inspiring thing. It is one of the most heartening forces in our national life. Its beneficent power is being evoked every day. The study of its motives, its ideals, and its operations should repay all who have the spiritual welfare, as well as the material welfare, of our people at heart. This is humanity's best hope for the future.

A FANTASY

Many of the great nations and peoples of the earth have developed, across the centuries, noteworthy characteristics or per-

sonalities which distinguish them and give them a definite place
in the perspective of history. In this long view, ancient Greece is
still the land of the intellect; ancient Rome, the land of empire
and law; medieval Italy, the land of art and beauty; Spain, the
land of gold and conquest; France, the land of sophistication and
gaiety; Germany, the land of stolid obedience to authority; and
England, the far-flung ruler of the seas.

America, with its vast reaches and mixed population, has not
yet assumed any such clear-cut character—although at the moment we are too often regarded by our fellow nations as "Mr.
Mass Production" or "Old Uncle Moneybags." This will pass, we
trust, when peace comes to the world and we no longer need to
hand out money and armaments to strengthen the free world
against Russian communism.

When we do cease to be the world's banker, what characteristic
will emerge in the long perspective as typically American? Will it
not be related to freedom—freedom *of* and *for* the individual—
"America, the land of the free"?

When the cross-country air traveler flies low enough he frequently sees painted on the rooftop of a large building the name
of a village or town. When the space traveler of the future
whooshes around the globe, he will see continents instead of villages. And, when he flies over America and looks down to identify
the continent, let us—in fancy—rearrange ourselves so that he will
at a glance know that it is indeed the Land of the Free—the land
of vast voluntary philanthropic enterprises. Suppose we arrange a
nation-wide landmark something like this:

First, let us put all the 265,000 churches of America side by side
in a great row from New York to San Francisco. They would
make a solid belt two hundred feet wide the whole width of the
continent, and there would be enough left to make another belt
of similar breadth from New Orleans to Duluth.

Let us then—in our further fancy—bring into one corner of
this enormous cross 1,158 private colleges and 12,000 private
schools, in a consolidated campus of 250,000 acres with approximately 45,000 buildings. They would just about cover the area
of Greater Chicago, and with about an equal population of
5,500,000 students and teachers.

In the opposite corner of the cross—covering the area of St.

Louis—would be another great patch of almost equal size containing our 3,169 voluntary hospitals. Perhaps the 50,000 nurses, doctors, specialists, and other employees could leave their 350,000 patients for a minute to wave to the cosmic visitor.

In order to be sure that "he who jets may read," let us ask the 6,000,000 boys and girls and young men and women who belong to all the private character-building agencies—such as the Boy Scouts, Girl Scouts, Y.M.C.A.'s, Y.W.C.A.'s, Catholic Youth groups, Y.M.H.A.'s, Y.W.H.A.'s, settlement houses, boys' clubs, and so on —to stand shoulder-to-shoulder and spell out the letters U.S.A. These letters would reach from Cheyenne, Wyoming, to Lake Michigan—standing 200 miles high.

Now our visitor knows he is passing over the U.S.A., but we still have not given him our key word—the distinctive characteristic of America that we want him to note. Let us spell it out for him. In order to do so, let's ask the 5,000,000 men and women who serve as workers each year in the various fund-raising campaigns of the 500,000 private institutions and agencies supported by voluntry philanthropy to join hands and form the letters of our key word—letters a hundred miles high, reading from El Paso, Texas, to Charleston, South Carolina. Here it is—the word that describes how the free men and women of America carry on their community life:

VOLUNTARILY

It is with this theme and with the institutions which have been created by voluntary philanthropy that this book deals.

ARNAUD C. MARTS

New York, N. Y.
August 15, 1953

PART ONE

What Is Philanthropy?

CHAPTER I

Philanthropy—The "Love of Mankind"

IN ITS simplest definition, philanthropy is the "love of mankind, especially as manifested in deeds of practical beneficence." It is that kind of "good will to men" which induces people to give voluntarily of their money, property, time, and strength to co-operative causes and institutions which serve the welfare, the health, the character, the mind, the soul, and the advancing culture of the human race.

A faithful search into the development of philanthropy would show that the evolution of this impulse is a true measuring rod of the development of civilization itself. We have come a long way from the attitude of the primitive native who naïvely shrugs, "Shall I starve while my sister has children she could sell?" to the attitude of the modern philanthropist who gives away millions of dollars with the comment, "Wealth is a sacred trust to be administered for the good of society."

The historian who would follow that long trail, as it traces for us the unfolding evolution of philanthropy, would shed revealing light on the essence of man's mind and spirit. Is it not that very spirit which a world-wide, godless, and ruthless attack is trying in our day to destroy!

It is important that Americans of our generation gain this third-dimensional insight into the mind and heart of American culture. During the past twenty years many have come to believe far too much in the power and obligation of the state to solve all the major problems of personal and social life. Constituted government at different levels should, of course, be given the power, to a reasonable degree, both to create and to guard the general conditions of a just and free society. But Americans, especially, should always remember that our greatest human advances have been pioneered by the voluntary endeavors of men and women to enrich and ennoble the life of their own communities.

One who attempts to interpret this story finds little enough attention paid to it by historians. For example, the author of a certain best seller, in which he paints the history of mankind in broad, swift strokes, takes us through 150 pages of the story—to the third century A.D.—before he once uses the word "charity." Even he, although consciously striving to interpret civilization in spiritual rather than military terms, seems to have ignored that quiet, unostentatious, yet persistent undertow—a developing sense of concern for the well-being of others—which has helped to draw humanity steadily onward toward a state of *co-operative civilization*.

In Ancient Times

Evidences of philanthropy leap out unexpectedly from the annals of even the earliest recorded civilizations. It is apparent that there have been men and women in every generation who have longed for a better day and who have been willing to aid the forces which they believed would hasten that day.

From the days of early recorded history, the Jews practiced an effective technique of philanthropy—the *tithe*. The tenth part of the yield of the harvest was to be given to the Lord, in support of religion and for the relief of the poor. Every seventh year, the people were required to let their fields lie fallow and the poor were permitted to garner the spontaneous growth during the sabbatical year. At every harvest a corner of each field was left unharvested for the poor. There are those today who feel that the tithe technique has not been improved upon and who earnestly urge a renewal of the practice.

The Pentateuch commanded charity for the unfortunate members of society and insisted that benevolence was a moral duty, not a matter of whimsical choice. All through the history of the Jewish race righteousness has found its most practical and fervid expression in charity. The "Cell of Silence," or "Chamber of Whispers," was a later Jewish technique which came near to being the ideal exercise of charity. This name was given to a quiet room in the synagogue into which the philanthropic stole, unobserved, and left donations for the respectable poor, who stole in—also unobserved—to obtain the help they needed.

The Jews have shown a sustained devotion to charity and philanthropy. They are no less generous than are the Christians of our nation, maintaining their race-old tradition in this respect. The new state of Israel was financed in its early and formative stages, to a large degree, by voluntary gifts of individual Jews throughout the world. American Jews contributed hundreds of millions of dollars to this endeavor to create a national Jewish homeland in Palestine.

About 450 B.C. the gentle Gautama—Buddha to us—established in India a religion based upon self-restraint and charity for the poor. Said Buddha: "In five ways should a clansman minister to his friends and familiars—by generosity, courtesy, and benevolence, by treating them as he treats himself, and by being as good as his word."

Two hundred years later we come upon the story of the first endowment of foreign missions. King Asoka was so impressed by the power of Gautama's simple code that he foreswore war, conquest, and greed, and devoted his wealth and influence to spreading the gospel of Buddha as he understood it. He sent missionaries into all parts of the civilized world—even to Persia, Greece, and Rome. He gave millions to endow Buddha's religion, and the consequences which have flowed from that philanthropy are incalculable.

One of the notable early examples of philanthropy was the gift of King Alexander, in the fourth century B.C., for the founding of Alexandria University in northern Egypt. In reality, this was a library which became a veritable storehouse of the wisdom, art, and skills of the past. Scholars came from all parts of the then Western World to consult its manuscripts and to exchange knowledge. Until it was destroyed by fire set by the Mohammedans, nearly a thousand years later, this monument to Alexander's philanthropy was the cultural center of the Mediterranean world.

Alexander's philanthropy also financed Aristotle's Lyceum so generously that at one time Aristotle is said to have had a thousand men scattered throughout Asia, Egypt, and Greece, seeking data for his writings on natural history.

IN THE CHRISTIAN ERA

The Christian era marked the inflow of a wholly new tide of unselfish concern for humanity. At the center of Jesus' teaching was the concept of one's responsibility for others. His appeal was addressed to all men of good will. He exhorted His followers, "Love thy neighbor as thyself," and He specifically prescribed charity to a certain rich young ruler as the very means of his salvation: "If thou wilt be perfect, go and sell that thou hast, and give to the poor."

EARLY CHRISTIAN PHILANTHROPIES

The thread of philanthropy seen so clearly in the life of the early Christian Church is the strand that leads directly to the far-flung efforts of the present generation in America.

The love of their fellow men seems to have been the key to the strength of the Christian Church during the first and second centuries. These people were utterly bewildering to the rulers and wise men of their day—as Gandhi has been in our day—for they coveted nothing for themselves. A Roman emperor said that one Christian missionary was worth more than a Roman legion in the penetration of barbaric Germany.

About A.D. 150 the Christians began to organize their charity work by creating in each church what they called a Church Fund, supported by voluntary gifts. Deacons then dispensed these funds to the needy. The early Christians believed, and demonstrated, that *the law of love is the law of life.*

Later, districts or deaconries were organized. In each district was a hospital, an alms office, an orphanage, and a shelter for babies. The hospital—or *Hôtel Dieu*—was at first not a hospital in our sense, but a place of *hospitality* for strangers.

In A.D. 321 Constantine gave license to give or bequeath money to the Church. From that time on substantial endowments began to accumulate around charitable institutions. As the late Frederick P. Keppel—long-time president of The Carnegie Corporation—put it in his book, *The Foundation*:

The endowment has its roots deep in human history. . . . The idea of permanent provision for worthy purposes fitted admirably into the ideals and practices of the Christian Church, and from the fourth century until the Reformation, practically all endowments were Church endowments.

These Church institutions—crude as they were—were lighthouses of civilization in those stormy centuries of cruelty and ignorance. "All through the darkest period of the Middle Ages," writes W. E. H. Lecky, in his *History of European Morals*, "amid ferocity and fanaticism and brutality, we may trace the subduing influence of Catholic charity blending strangely with every excess of violence and every outburst of persecution. Charitable habits, even when formed in the first instance from selfish motives, even when so directed as to be positively injurious to the recipient, rarely fail to exercise a softening and purifying influence on character."

HOSPITALS

Two of our noblest modern institutions—the hospital and the university—evolved slowly from early Christian charities. At first the hospital was a rest room, or hospitalium, in the house of the bishop—with the bishop himself, according to Harnack, required to act as physician. The first documentary proof of a hospital is of one established at Caesarea in A.D. 369 by St. Basil. It seems to have been a veritable city, with pavilions for various diseases and residences for physicians, nurses, and convalescents. St. Gregory called it a "heaven on earth."

Following the Crusades, hospitals multiplied at an astonishing rate throughout Europe and England. At one time there were attached to the churches and religious orders literally thousands of hospitals for lepers alone. Revenue was derived chiefly from Church appropriations, private bequests, and endowments. The endowments of some hospitals extended to farms, vineyards, houses, and even whole villages.

The jousting tournament—of which Sir Walter Scott's description has thrilled every schoolboy—was often staged as a benefit for a medieval hospital. Lasting a week or a fortnight, this brilliant carnival of sport, like a modern charity ball, would yield a handsome financial return. Also, various societies and guilds, to which people contributed membership fees, were established in support of hospitals.

UNIVERSITIES

During the Dark Ages, universities began to spring up at these centers of religion and charity, and the dying embers of learning were again fanned into flame by men with a "love of mankind." The early universities were not created by rulers or by the rich. In the beginning they were modest affairs, looked down upon with scorn by the nobles. Created by the middle class for the middle class, they stand as a perfect illustration of how people may work together in a voluntary endeavor for the good of all.

Important universities were founded in about this order: Salerno, 850; Bologna, 1088; Paris, 1130. Following a quarrel among the founders of the University of Paris, some of them crossed the Channel and founded Oxford in 1150 and Cambridge in 1190— probably after a quarrel at Oxford. Then came Padua in 1222 and Salamanca in 1234.

Out of the Universities of Oxford and Paris, about 1240, came a young man who, if he had been the *only* product of these two institutions, would have repaid their founders for all the efforts invested. His name was Roger Bacon. "Cease to be ruled by dogmas and authorities; look at the world," he cried, and the age of dry and sterile debate began to yield to the modern age of science, of creative thought, and of invention.

CATHEDRALS

One must not forget those other majestic creations of the medieval Christian Church—the cathedrals. They too, of course, were largely voluntary undertakings.

Funds for their creation were provided in many ways. A state, a city, or a monarch might make a grant from the public treasury; the bishop might provide the funds; the people might be appealed to for contributions; or the funds might be raised by a combination of these and other methods. All the great cathedrals were, in part at least, built by freely donated labor. At times—as when heavy masonry was to be lifted to the towering spires—the people of the whole countryside would drop their work, for days or weeks at a stretch, to carry and haul and pull at the ropes. Some of these massive structures were two and three hundred years in the building. When completed, they became the great repositories of Christian art—treasure houses of the finest paintings, sculpture, stained glass, tapestries, and precious metals produced by the European masters. For centuries they were undoubtedly the central factor in the cultivation of the Western World's appreciation of the arts.

H. G. Wells, summing up in his *Outline of History* the progress of the human race, pays this eloquent tribute to the love of mankind which we have been endeavoring to trace:

It is only within the last three or at most four thousand years that we have any clear evidence that voluntary self-abandonment to some greater end, without fee or reward, was an acceptable idea to men, or that anyone propounded it. Then we find spreading over the surface of human affairs, as patches of sunshine spread and pass over the hillsides on a windy day in spring, the idea that there is a happiness in self-devotion greater than any personal gratification or triumph, and a life of mankind different and greater and more important than the sum of all individual lives within it.

We have seen that idea become vivid as a beacon, vivid as sunshine caught and reflected dazzlingly by some window in the landscape, in the teaching of Buddha, Lao Tse, and, most clearly of all, of Jesus of Nazareth.

Through all its variations and corruptions Christianity has never completely lost the suggestion of a devotion to God's commonweal that makes the personal pomp of monarchs and rulers seem like the insolence of an overdressed servant and the splendors and gratifications of wealth like the waste of robbers. No man living in a community which such a religion as Christianity or Islam has touched can be altogether a slave; there is an ineradicable quality to these religions that compels men to judge their masters and to realize their own responsibility to the world.

In the Western World: The Planting of an Acorn

In order to bridge the centuries, let me recall a philanthropic deed in England recorded in the year 1584—the consequences of which soon spanned the ocean, and still influence our daily lives in America.

Sir Walter Mildmay, a name rarely encountered, did not achieve sufficient distinction to be noticed by historians, but he rendered a service of which some of his more famous contemporaries could well have been proud.

Sir Walter was Chancellor of the Exchequer under Queen Elizabeth, and for a time one of her favorites. When she once chided him for an absence from Court and demanded an explanation, Sir Walter—a bit reticent and cryptic in his responses—replied, "Madame, I have been away planting an acorn, and when it becomes an oak, God only knoweth what it will amount to."

The acorn he had planted was Emmanuel College at Cambridge University. Probably the reason for reticence in explaining his act more fully was that the new college was founded for the Puritan sect and Queen Bess was not a Puritan. The college kindled a new zeal for freedom in the souls of its graduates. Soon they began to migrate to America, where the acorn found itself the progenitor of a burgeoning forest of democracy and liberalism in the New World. Dr. Charles F. Thwing, late president of Western Reserve University, once said: "From Emmanuel College came the founders of Harvard, the founders of New England and, in a special sense, the founders of a new nation."

The Reverend John Harvard was one of the early graduates of Emmanuel. He came to New England at the age of twenty-nine, and with other "Godly Gentlemen and lovers of learning" planned a college which would advance learning in their new home. Two years later he died, leaving his library and one half his small estate to the proposed college. With this aid the institution was soon founded, receiving his name, and in 1642 the first class was graduated from Harvard College—only twenty-two years after the landing of the *Mayflower*. The acorn was growing fast.

Nor did it stop growing when Harvard College was established. These same Puritans and their descendants—Congregationalists, we call them—carried their zeal for education and their passionate "love of mankind" into every section of the nation which they penetrated. In 1701 they founded Yale; in 1769, Dartmouth. In 1793, they established a college in what they termed the "West"— Williams; in 1821, Amherst; a few years later they were out in Ohio where they founded Western Reserve in 1826, Oberlin in 1833, and Marietta in 1835. In 1837 they established Knox in Illinois; in 1844, Olivet in Michigan; in 1846, Beloit in Wisconsin and Grinnell in Iowa; in 1853, Washington in Missouri; Washburn in Kansas in 1865; Pomona in California, 1887. Each of these institutions was founded by personal efforts and private gifts, often in tiny amounts scraped together, with great sacrifice, from the most varied sources. No taxes were assessed to establish or support them. All were expressions of the consuming desire of men and women to provide liberal, Christian education for the sons and daughters of a new nation.

Today, the accumulated financial resources of the institutions named, which are but a few of the direct offshoots in America of the acorn Sir Walter Mildmay planted 350 years ago, at Cambridge, England, exceed $500,000,000—all accrued from voluntary gifts and all dedicated to the advancement of learning and character.

Of the spiritual and cultural values which cannot be entered on the books of mankind in terms of dollars, it is quite impossible to speak at all adequately. A roster of the men and women who have been educated at these institutions and at the hundreds of other colleges and schools which were founded by their graduates would read like a *Who's Who* in the fields of government, religion, education, the arts, and business.

Among the many leaders of our nation who were trained in colleges which grew directly or collaterally from this acorn have been Samuel Adams, John Adams, Thomas Jefferson, Daniel Webster, James Russell Lowell, Theodore Roosevelt, William Howard Taft, Calvin Coolidge, Franklin Roosevelt, Charles M. Hall, Robert A. Millikan, the Compton brothers, and Charles Evans Hughes. By any reckoning, we shall not be accused of over-enthusiasm if we say that Sir Walter made a good investment for mankind when he gave the money to found Emmanuel College. It was a philanthropy which was to have a profound effect upon the shape of our whole modern world.

AMERICAN PHILANTHROPY HAS SET NEW STANDARDS

In the United States—especially in the twentieth century— the forces and forms of voluntary philanthropic endeavor have reached their fullest development. We have long been known as the most generous nation of all time. Today, our philanthropies not only cover the nation but girdle the globe. No such fabric of voluntary organizations has ever been known. It would be hard to overestimate the part they have played not only in setting the high standards of our community life, but in creating the spiritual climate in which our people and our country have grown up.

Many circumstances have combined to produce this result. Our shores were settled by devout Christians; and religion is the fountainhead of philanthropy. These people knew deprivation and struggle; and hardships breed sympathy and mutual helpfulness. The enormity of their tasks taught them unexampled cooperation. They had a burning desire for freedom and independence; this spirit gave them the courage and the initiative to develop all sorts of self-directed activities for the fuller realization of that freedom. The distance of the colonists from the mother country threw them on their own resources. If they wanted a church or a school or a college, they had to build it.

Families that had risked everything to gain political and religious liberty were not simply seeking freedom *from* tyranny and dependence, but liberty *for* the building of a fuller life. It was this freedom-loving and voluntary spirit, self-confident, cooperative, and immensely creative, that built the real America with its network of churches, colleges, libraries, hospitals, and all the humanitarian agencies that have helped to make the American dream come true.

These immensely practical expressions of good will have made our country—to millions of less fortunate people in every corner of the earth—the Promised Land. In these latter days many have learned to their sorrow that *there is no philanthropy under a dictator*. Hitler abolished even such a harmless organization as the Boy Scouts. Stalin was bitter in his attitude toward voluntary efforts by the people. Mao Tse-tung is ruthlessly expelling from China the churches, the Christian colleges, and the Y.M.C.A. *Where God is not recognized, neither is the love of fellow men.* As Senator John W. Bricker put it in a recent statement: "The American citizen derives his freedom from God, the Creator, not from his government, while the citizens of many other countries have only such freedom as their government chooses to grant."

Philanthropy and the protection of freedom go hand in hand. Both, we have ample reason to believe, have reached their fullest development in America. For years it has been our privilege to lead the world in many forms of philanthropic activity, and to share the results of such activity with less favored nations.

Would it not be a tragic turning backward and a renunciation of our birthright if—following the false mirage of authoritarian, governmental provision for the total welfare of our citizens—we were in the slightest degree to slacken the voluntary philanthropies which have given our nation its most distinctive, most kindly, character?

From the chapters that follow it will be evident that I do not for a moment believe that this will happen. As we shall see, such faith in the American people has ample foundation.

CHAPTER II

Stories of Notable Givers

T HIS thing of giving," said George F. Burba, "I do not understand, any more than you do, but there is something about it that blesses us. . . . Those who give most, have most left. . . . I believe that everyone who dries a tear will be spared the shedding of a thousand tears. . . . I believe that every sacrifice we make will so enrich us in the future that our regret will be that we did not sacrifice the more. . . .

"Give—and somewhere, from out the clouds, or from the sacred depths of human hearts, a melody divine will reach your ears, and gladden all your days upon the earth."

One day I sat in the parlor of an eighty-year-old friend who had just made a gift of $100,000 to a college, and who was experiencing the usual exhilaration of such an act. Suddenly he pointed to a man of his own age who was walking by. "See that old coot?" he said. "He has the same amount of money I have, but I feel sorry for him, poor chap."

"Why?" I asked.

"Because he has never learned how to buy any happiness with his money. All his life he has played one game. It has been his lifetime game to be worth more on December 31st of each year than he was on January 1st. So far as I know, he has won that little game every year. Now he's eighty—and he's miserable. Think what fun he could have if he'd only given away a little of his money now and then to help his fellow men. Too bad! Poor old man! Too bad!"

What, indeed, is it that inspires a man to take a substantial sum from his private capital and freely give it into the treasury of a philanthropic institution for the service of others?

Some men give again and again. Others seem incapable of doing so, though their possessions may have become a source of re-

14

sponsibility and anxiety. Some know how to give both liberally and wisely, and derive deep satisfaction from the results. Others form the habit of keeping all they possess, and appear pleased at having been able to resist the temptation to give. They often manage to persuade themselves either that the cause is foolish, or none of their concern. Cynicism supports such an attitude.

But what are the motives that lead to giving?

Raymond Moley says something in his book, *How to Keep Our Liberty*, that applies in this connection, although he is speaking of political action by citizens in support of "nonmaterial" American ideals:

People are moved by many impulses other than those with roots in stomachs and pocketbooks. Human beings are endowed with the sentiments of idealism, loyalty and pride associated with the home, the family, the local community, friends, ancestry, tradition, religion and patriotism.

Evidently they must be rooted deep in human nature.

If we recount the stories of a few notable gifts that have become a part of the fiber of our nation, it may shed light on the motive power behind benevolent giving.

A BOY FROM MAINE

Gardner Colby was a boy whose seagoing father had died leaving his widow—scarcely twenty-five years of age—with a family of four and no means for their support. The ten-year-old Gardner was earning a few pennies by working in a potash plant in Waterville, Maine.

Also in Waterville was a new-born college, chartered as the Maine Literary and Theological Institution, whose first president, the Reverend Dr. Chaplin, was a kindly man who befriended and aided the little Colby family. In 1820, when the institution celebrated the erection of its first building, the whole village joined in the jubilation. A lighted candle was placed in each of the many windows in the front of the building and the villagers looked on the spectacle with awe. It was a sight to thrill a youth befriended by the president of this wonderful institution.

Then the little family moved away to struggle and advance

elsewhere. Gardner prospered—first as a small merchant, then as a wholesale merchant, an importer, a manufacturer, a railroad president, and a capitalist.

One Sabbath morning as he sat in his church pew in Massachusetts, a chance word from the preacher strangely moved him. To illustrate a point, the minister recalled an episode from his early life—the picture of Dr. Chaplin coming bowed and dejected from the home of a wealthy man in Portland, repeating over and over, "God save Waterville College! Waterville College must not perish!" Before his death Dr. Chaplin's efforts had indeed saved the college for the time being, but by 1864 the ravages of the Civil War had so reduced its resources that it seemed as if nothing short of Providence could prevent its closing.

At the next commencement season Gardner Colby came to Waterville with a message. He offered the college $50,000 for endowment on condition that $100,000 be obtained from other friends. In two years' time the gift was claimed. Some years later Waterville College became known as Colby College.

What led this New Englander to give so generously while all about him others were easily evading the same appeals? Was the motive power compounded of childhood memories of a valiant mother, or of gratitude, or of an inner desire to give evidence to the people of Waterville that the poor young widow and her family had in them the stuff that wins? Above and through it all, was there not a deep-rooted love of God and mankind?

IN THE SOUTH

General Samuel C. Armstrong had a firm philosophy: it was "Subtract hard work from life and in a few months it will all have gone to pieces. Labor—next to the grace of God in the heart—is the greatest promoter of morality, the greatest power for civilization." It was his philosophy and his vision that gave new direction to Negro education in the South with the establishment, in 1868, of Hampton Institute in Virginia—an institution destined to prove of incalculable consequence to the Negro race and to the total pattern of American social life.

General Armstrong was the son of a Congregational missionary

to Hawaii who had learned, from his observation of educational
work there, practical methods which might be applied to the
training of a race totally unfamiliar with the academic educational process. With the financial aid of the American Missionary
Society, Hampton Institute offered Negro youths instruction of
an intensely practical sort. It comprised training in the most
common and useful forms of labor—helping the Negro to fit
himself for life in spheres where he was most likely to live it.

In 1881 Booker T. Washington, a graduate of Hampton Institute, founded Tuskegee Institute in Alabama, fashioning his
school after Hampton. Before long fifteen smaller institutions
sprang up as offshoots of Tuskegee. Thus, the new lead which
philanthropy at Hampton had given furnished the direction and
drive for the main educational efforts in behalf of the Negro
race for the next half century.

In the same year that General Armstrong established Hampton
another man took a great step in aiding education in the South.
Imagine the moral influence of George Peabody's act, in 1867,
in establishing the Peabody Education Fund with an initial gift
of $3,000,000—and much more added later—with his statement
that the purpose was to re-establish an educational system in the
South for both white and black.

The announcement of this gift had a profound influence in
assuaging public passions. To make the announcement, Mr. Peabody wisely called together at Washington a group of the most
distinguished men of both North and South. In the Brady photograph of the conference we see General Grant standing side by
side with Governor Aiken of South Carolina, and Winthrop of
the Federal Congress and Rives of the Confederate Congress sit-
ting side by side.

Here is a contemporary account of the meeting:

After reading his deed of gift to them for the children of the South,
there is a solemn hush, and then it is proposed that the blessings of
Almighty God be called upon this solemn act. They kneel there in a
circle of prayer—the Puritan of New England, the pioneer of the
West, the financier of the metropolis, and the defeated veterans of the
Confederacy. With bended knee and touching elbow, they dedicate

this great gift. They consecrate themselves to the task of its wise
expenditure. In that act and in that moment, not quite two years after
Appomattox, is the first guaranty of a reunited country.

Others took up the cause of Negro education. John F. Slater of
Connecticut made a gift of a million dollars in 1882; Daniel Hand,
also of Connecticut, gave a like amount in 1888. Starting in 1902,
the Rockefeller family began a system of giving to Negro education that has approximated a hundred million dollars. There
were also large gifts from Andrew Carnegie and his Foundation.
In 1917, Julius Rosenwald of Chicago contributed more than
fifteen million dollars; and during the 1920 decade there were
gifts and bequests of millions of dollars from George Eastman
of Rochester and scores of other philanthropists. Rarely has there
been a nobler outpouring of devoted gifts for a single cause, continuing to this very day.

A MICHIGAN PIONEER

Here is a story worth notice—not because it is extraordinary,
but because it is so natural, so typical, so indigenous to America.

Edward K. Warren was born in 1847 in a village parsonage in
Vermont. While still a lad, the family moved to Michigan—
recently admitted to statehood and very much a pioneer region.
The vigorous father presided over "home missionary" churches.
The equally vigorous son was raised on the three R's, a fourth
R—religion—and lots of hard work.

While running a country store, where he learned that whale-
bone was getting scarce, and that the bone in women's corsets
had an uncomfortable habit of breaking, he invented an inex-
pensive and flexible substitute made out of the springy quills
of turkey feathers. He named it "featherbone." He got a mechanic
to help design machinery, and in 1883 set up a little factory in
his home town of Three Oaks.

For a while it was tough sledding. One day when things looked
dark he promised the Lord that if He would see him through this
financial crisis, he would "tithe" for the rest of his life. Young
Warren came through, and set to work tithing and working with
the Lord in any way he could. He seems to have taken as an
everyday motto, "Let us do with our might what our hands find
to do."

The business prospered, and the profits began to bear fruit in many directions. Mr. Warren helped to rebuild the local Congregational Church and remained its lifelong pillar. Tremendously interested in Sunday Schools, he boosted the work of the International Sunday School Association, became its president, and organized the international convention in Jerusalem in 1904.

Loving his village, his region, and his state, he steadily expanded his interests and activities. The factory was the chief source of his fellow townsmen's livelihood. His bank and his store and his farm rendered useful service. He acquired large holdings of native woods and dunes shoreland along Lake Michigan, setting up a Warren Foundation to look after their use. Before his death he had the satisfaction of giving an assembly site and buildings to the Congregational Church for summer conventions. Warren's Woods—a tract of primeval forest—was later deeded to the State of Michigan as a laboratory for the botany department of the University of Michigan and for the general use of all students and the public. There has also been set up in perpetuity a Dunes State Park for the enjoyment and education of the people of Michigan, also by deed to the state.

Finally Mr. Warren conceived the idea of gathering together in a folksy sort of museum, located in Three Oaks, every possible relic and reminder of the local pioneer civilization that he and his father had seen develop. He visited other museums like that of the University of Wisconsin, got expert help, and realized his dream. Now, some years after his death, this unique collection is being moved to Lansing—given to Michigan State College.

If these acts are called philanthropic, to him they were as natural as raising and caring for his own family. Many such men and women—never celebrated in national news columns—have lived similar fruitful lives, passing on the by-products to their fellow citizens.

North Carolina Farm Boy

In the year 1856 there was born on a farm in North Carolina a boy who was to give $80,000,000 to philanthropy, and to find in his giving the supreme happiness of a life of many triumphs.

Let us go back to "Buck" Duke's parents and to the father

whose homely maxims James B. Duke quoted all through his life. The father, Washington Duke, started as a hard-working farmer near Durham, North Carolina. Only six months of his life had been spent in school. A man of the utmost integrity and good native intelligence, he was deeply loyal to the Methodist Church and its ministry. Religion was a vital part of his life. James Duke said in later years: "My old Daddy always said that if he amounted to anything in life, it was due to the Methodist circuit riders who so often visited his home, and whose preaching and counsel brought out the best that was in him. If I amount to anything in this world I will owe it to my Daddy and to the Methodist Church."

When the Civil War was ended, Washington Duke returned to his family to find he had lost everything and that his Confederate money was worthless. All he had left were two blind army mules which had been given him, fifty cents, and a small shanty for shelter. His daughter Mary was housed with the neighbors, and Washington and his two sons, Buck and Ben, slept in the shed. There they discovered that the soldiers had overlooked something—a quantity of good leaf tobacco. And in an old log barn the Dukes started their first factory, pulverizing the tobacco with flails and proudly labeling the bags of prepared tobacco *Pro Bono Publico*.

Loading the *Pro Bono* onto a covered wagon drawn by the two blind mules, the father and his two sons began an itinerant life of bartering at the crossroads. When Buck was eight years old another of his duties was to load a bag of grain on a mule's back and carry it to the mill to be ground into flour. The water slipping through the millrace entranced him, and he lay in the grass by the hour watching the water pour over the big wheel. He longed to own a water mill.

Soon the tobacco business was a great success and the three children were sent away to college—Buck going to Eastman Business College in Poughkeepsie, New York, where he worked day and night with boundless enthusiasm. At fourteen, he was made the manager of his father's factory; at eighteen, he was admitted to partnership; and by the age of thirty he was in New York, opening up a vast new market.

And now he had time for that boyhood dream—water power. His experiments in harnessing the swift waters of his native state resulted in vast power developments and ever-greater revenue for the Duke fortune.

The father's interests were turning to a small Methodist institution in Randolph, North Carolina—Trinity College. In 1890, Washington Duke offered $85,000 for a set of new buildings, *if* the little college would move to Durham. The move was made and Mr. Duke gave hundreds of thousands of dollars to Trinity before his death in 1905.

His son Buck continued to give lavish sums to Trinity, realizing, as he did so, a lifelong desire to serve God and humanity. Prompted by intense love for his father, deep loyalty to the Church, and patriotic attachment to his state, he set up the great Duke Endowment of approximately $40,000,000 for the betterment of the institutions and the people of the Carolinas. In particular, he provided vast sums for a university to be named after his father, Washington Duke. Trinity College was expanded into Duke University to meet the conditions of the gift.

Thus, the swiftly moving waters of his native state turn the wheels of productive industry and earn, year after year, the funds which bring education and well-being to the people of his own beloved section of America. They build homes for orphans, they help build and maintain rural Methodist churches, they provide pensions for aged Methodist circuit riders, and thus establish a living monument of eternal service to Washington Duke.

SCIENTIFIC GENIUS FROM OHIO

Charles M. Hall, son of a Congregational minister, was born in 1864 and spent his youth in the little college town of Oberlin, Ohio. He was a studious, earnest boy, deeply interested in chemistry and inventions. As a lad, he fell into the habit of seeking out the college's professor of chemisty, F. F. Jewett. He would come to buy a few cents' worth of tubing or test tubes or other experimental material, and then disappear to carry on his private experiments at home.

When later he entered the college as a student, Professor Jewett quickly recognized the unusual quality of his work, and soon they were working side by side, exploring the mysteries of chemistry.

One day Professor Jewett said to his students, "If anyone should invent a process by which aluminum could be made on a commercial scale, not only would he be a benefactor to the world, but he would also be able to lay up for himself a great fortune."

Young Hall was thrilled by the challenge. Patiently he worked at the problem throughout college. With the help and encouragement of Professor Jewett, he rigged up one electric battery after another and tried every variation of method, until one morning after graduation—in the woodshed laboratory he had fitted out at home—he discovered the secret of producing aluminum on a commercial scale. Upon this epoch-making invention was built a vast, essential industry and, inevitably, a sizable fortune.

Charles Hall early began to turn the overflow of his energy and means to the service of his Alma Mater, serving on its board of trustees and making numerous and continued gifts toward its expanding program. His interests outside business covered a wide cultural range—religion, education, music, and the fine arts. He turned over his personal art collection to Oberlin.

He died young and unmarried—just under fifty—and left his great estate in three parts: one to Oberlin; one to Berea College in Kentucky; and one to education and missions in the Orient, a work dear to the hearts of his parents.

Oberlin's share set the college on the road to a position of substantial endowment and expanded influence. Thus, the lad who found his inspiration and his help in the modest little brick laboratory blessed his Alma Mater with a matchless gift out of the abundance which his genius and her influence had created.

THE SECRET PARTNER

Another notable story appeared, with the above title, in *Time* magazine of August 4, 1952, under the section devoted to philanthropy. The story was also featured, with pictures, in *Life*.

According to the account in *Time*, Claud H. Foster of Cleveland, a retired inventor-manufacturer who recently gave away $4,000,000, lays his business successes to the fact that if you are "in tune with the secret partner, He'll do something for you." The secret partner, of course, is God. Foster expressed himself as feeling strongly that "something was done for him" quite beyond his own efforts.

The account mentioned three instances. At fourteen, he had phenomenal success with four acres of early potatoes, which providentially were spared any frost, brought $1,800, and enabled him to pay off a debt that had haunted his father for years.

At nineteen—strangely combining his skills as a machinist and a self-taught trombone player—he invented an auto horn that worked off the exhaust and gave out several musical notes. This "Gabriel Horn" made him $150,000.

Then he hit upon the big thing—a shock absorber for autos. Here, again, the idea seemed to come to him out of the blue, as he watched a boat approaching a dock. As he now recalls it, his attention was directed by his secret partner "to a workman who was wrapping a rope around a pile, snubbing the boat." It gave him the idea for the first successful auto shock absorber—the Gabriel Snubber. The company expanded and netted him a million dollars a year, and brought an offer of ten million dollars which he turned down, saying the company was not worth that much. He later sold out for $4,000,000 and retired to spend much of his time in a $3,500 house he built on the shore of Lake Erie.

Here is the last chapter of the story as told by *Time*:

The Big Surprise. Since Foster felt he had only been the instrument of his partner in making his fortune, he gave much of it away. But he still thought he had too much, since "my needs are small." Last week Foster invited many of his old friends—along with representatives of educational and charitable institutions—to a party in Cleveland's Hotel Statler. He promised them the "surprise of your life."

After they had all dined well on filet mignon, Foster arose. One by one the representatives of fifteen Jewish, Catholic and Protestant charitable institutions and Western Reserve University were asked to step to the head table, where Foster sat with a happy smile on his face. At the table each one was handed a big check or a batch of securities. When the give-away party was all over, Foster had handed out $4,000,000.

Said he: "Too many institutions get their money from dead men. I wanted to see them get it. I have no more use for the money. You can take it all, but leave me my friends."

IN THE STATE OF PENNSYLVANIA

Why do men give? For many reasons. We find some of the answers in these notable cases of generosity. And here I want to add one more story—that of a man who said to the author, "You give *your time*, and I'll give *my money*."

In 1935, when the trustees of Bucknell University persuaded me to become part-time president after I had declined election as president, I agreed to spend Thursday and Friday of each week at the college in Lewisburg, Pennsylvania, while continuing my duties as president of the firm of Marts and Lundy, Inc., in New York City.

Like many other colleges in the 1930's, Bucknell was suffering acutely from lack of funds, and I early asked the members of the board of trustees to help me find new supporters for the college. A trustee, Senator Andrew J. Sordoni of Wilkes-Barre, immediately thought of a neighbor: seventy-five-year-old Daniel C. Roberts, retired official of the Woolworth Company. Mr. Roberts, as a boy in Watertown, New York, had been a clerk in the same general store where Frank and Charles Woolworth, Fred Kirby, Frederick Weckesser, Seymour Knox, and other creators of the modern mass-merchandising chain store were clerks, and together they had built the great Woolworth chain. Mr. Roberts and I were introduced.

A friendship sprang up, and with it new plans for the development and strengthening of Bucknell. The main college building had burned down in 1932 and still lay in ashes, a capital debt of $700,000 hung over us, and the institution was operating at a sizable deficit. Mr. Roberts soon came to understand and appreciate the president's efforts to bring new life and resources to the college while at the same time carrying his own business responsibilities in New York City. One day he invited me to lunch. And, as luncheons go, this proved to be no ordinary date.

When it was over Mr. Roberts asked me to go down to the bank with him. There he handed over to me Woolworth stock worth $100,000. He had committed an act of faith. With this help, we were able to raise the other $300,000 needed to rebuild Old Main.

Not long afterward I was invited to lunch with him again,

and again was given securities worth $100,000—with which to hack away at the mountain of debt, which was completely paid off a few years later. Mr. Roberts next gave $150,000 toward a gymnasium. Then a new engineering building had to be built in order to gain accreditation for Bucknell's engineering departments, and Mr. Roberts responded with $250,000, again in stocks, toward that objective.

About that time the pressure of double duties upon me was becoming heavy. I was expecting to relinquish the Bucknell duties, when without warning at a college chapel service a petition was presented to me—signed by each of Bucknell's 1,200 students—urging me to continue as president. The next day Mr. Roberts repeated this urging and said, "Let's you and me help those Bucknell boys and girls—you give your time, and I'll give my money."

During the next two years, before his death, he gave another $250,000, which helped to build the Ellen Clark Bertrand Library dedicated in 1951, and several thousands more for the Bucknell Junior College (now Wilkes College) at Wilkes-Barre. In five short years he had become the largest single benefactor of this century-old Pennsylvania college.

Before he died in 1940 he said to me, "You helped me invest my money in young people while I was still alive and could see it at work. You have brought me some of the greatest happiness of my whole life."

When I retired from the presidency of Bucknell in 1945, and the trustees expressed appreciation for the progress made, I stated that most of this would have been quite impossible except for Daniel C. Roberts. It was an honor to be able to say: "To the modest, generous gentleman, Daniel C. Roberts, who backed me with his gifts and who thus encouraged many other friends to make generous gifts also, and who would not even permit me to reveal his name until it became absolutely necessary to do so, Bucknell owes an incalculable debt of gratitude."

Today, on the Bucknell campus, the central building of Old Main is named the Daniel C. Roberts Hall—a name which will remain on the lips of thousands of young Americans for generations to come as they walk in and out of this beautiful building in their quest for growth of mind and spirit.

PART TWO

What Are Its Chief Fruits?

CHAPTER III

America's Private Colleges

PERHAPS no product of voluntary philanthropy deserves more careful study than the American college. And for several reasons. Its philanthropic ancestry is unusually clear, as can be seen in familiar examples. The small private institution —independent of tax support—is still our typical college, humorously and affectionately celebrated for generations as "Old Siwash" or "The College on the Hill." These schools are among our oldest and best beloved. Their influence on our developing nation has been beyond all calculation. Woven into the finest traditions of region, locality, and family, they have been living fountains of liberal education. Though still inaccurately called "private," they stand out among our most devoted public servants. Their influence was never greater, nor the ceaseless calls upon them.

"First the blade, and then the ear . . ." The seeds of higher education in America were hopefully planted by the religious zeal and far-sighted wisdom of educational pioneers who made, and secured, voluntary gifts of money, goods, and energy for the establishment of our earliest academies and colleges. During the past hundred years there has been a magnificent development of state universities, so that every state in the Union now has one or more public institutions of higher learning. But the colleges, universities, and professional schools which are self-supporting and under the administration of independent boards of trustees are still vastly in the majority—1,217 of the total of 1,865 institutions of higher learning. Higher education has by no means been taken out of the hands of private philanthropy and assumed by the state to the same degree as have our high schools and grade schools.

COLONIAL ORIGINS

Ten of our present colleges were founded prior to the Revolution, all by private philanthropy: Harvard in 1636; William and Mary, 1693; St. John's at Annapolis, 1696; Yale, 1701; University of Pennsylvania, 1740; Princeton, 1746; Columbia in 1754; Brown, 1764; Rutgers, 1766; Dartmouth, 1769. Of these ten, only William and Mary, the University of Pennsylvania, and Rutgers are now partially supported by tax appropriations.

But it should not be supposed that these early institutions received no help whatsoever from the early governments of colony and town; for their founders naturally appealed to every possible source of support, including the political authorities. At times they received various grants of land or money and, in some instances, even had special temporary taxes laid in their behalf.

During Harvard's early difficulties we read, for instance, of the town of Portsmouth, New Hampshire, in 1669, appropriating £60 per year for seven years—in response "to the loud groans of the sinking college." This beneficence of the citizens of Portsmouth was gratefully remembered at Harvard for generations. Before Yale was founded, Harvard was supported by citizens of the Colonies in Connecticut as well as by Massachusetts; and the lawmakers there devised a sort of voluntary taxation which was not enforced as strictly as the compulsory taxes. They ordained that two men in every town should be appointed "who shall demand that every family shall give toward the support of Harvard College," and who should suggest that a half bushel of corn would be about the right contribution. Technically, this was still a gift!

VOLUNTARY AND INDEPENDENT

However, in spite of this welcome help produced by grants from government, the initiative for our early independent colleges was assumed by men acting in a purely voluntary capacity, and almost the entire financial burden of maintaining them was borne by philanthropy. Gifts came in all sizes and from all conditions of people. Edwin G. Dexter, in his *History of the United*

States, quotes this description of some of the early gifts to Harvard:

We read of a number of sheep bequeathed by one man, a quantity of cotton cloth with 9s. presented by another; a pewter flagon worth 10s. by a third; a fine dish, a sugar spoon, a silver-tipt jug, one great salt, one small trencher salt by others; and of presents of legacies amounting severally to 5s, £1, £2, etc. What, in fact, were those humble benefactions?—They were contributions from the *res augusta domi,* from pious, virtuous, enlightened penury to the noblest of all causes—the advancement of education.

And Professor Jesse Brundage Sears, in his study of philanthropy in *The History of American Higher Education,* tells also of several sizable gifts to Harvard prior to 1700:

During the next few decades several gifts of £100 were received, and in 1650 Richard Saltonstall, of England, gave "to the college" goods and money worth 320 pounds sterling. In 1680 Sir Matthew Holworthy bequeathed "to be disposed of by the directors as they shall judge best for the promotion of learning and promulgation of the Gospel" £1,000. The Honorable William Stoughton erected a building in 1699 which cost £1,000 Massachusetts currency.

A VIRGINIA STORY—WILLIAM AND MARY

Some of our present-day private colleges grow impatient if they are unable to put a million-dollar-campaign through to complete success within a few months; but in the early days no such speed was even imagined. In the case of the College of William and Mary, it took seventy-four years to accumulate sufficient funds for its final establishment. This nearly century-long campaign effort started in 1619 when Sir Edwin Sandys, treasurer of the London Company, which was colonizing Virginia, recommended to the English Parliament that a grant of 15,000 acres be made for the establishment of an Episcopal college in Virginia. The grant was made, and King James I then appealed to the churches for contributions of money. Interest was aroused and £1,500 subscribed. Others gave books and materials. Two

English crews took up collections for the proposed college—totaling £67—and a bequest of £300 was received.

In 1622, just as the college was about to be launched, Indians stormed down upon the James River settlement and killed hundreds of white men, including the superintendent of the proposed school. The founding was postponed, and the money and property put in care of trustees to await a more propitious time. If this Indian massacre had not occurred, William and Mary would have earned the honor of being America's first college—for in 1622 John Harvard was still a student at Emmanuel College in Cambridge, England, and not a step had yet been taken to establish the institution that was later to bear his name.

In 1660 the idea of the college in Virginia was revived, this time by the Colony's own settlers. Subscriptions for the purpose of launching the school were sought from every class and in every amount. This phase of the campaign was waged continuously for the next thirty years. From time to time gifts and bequests were added to the fund.

Finally, in 1688, certain wealthy planters of the Colony made up a subscription fund of £2,500 and sent the Reverend James Blair to England to present the matter at Court. Dr. Blair, by the way, was a graduate of Harvard, which was already sending out men competent to lead in the cultural and educational enterprises of the growing colonies. The good man succeeded in obtaining a charter from King William and Queen Mary and, in addition, both of them gave generously—even against the vigorous and profane protests of their attorney general.

Twenty thousand acres of land were given with the charter; a tax of a penny a pound was laid, in behalf of the college, on all tobacco to be exported from Virginia and Maryland; and the fees and profits from the surveyor general's office of Virginia were appropriated to the support of the new institution. Because of this royal generosity, the new college, which had been named William and Mary—enjoying an annual revenue of £4,000—was for half a century far richer than Harvard.

During the Revolutionary war its buildings were burned, its library lost, and it was shorn of its prestige and much of its property through the disestablishment of the Church in Virginia, which Jefferson and Madison brought about at that time. Not until 150 years later—when John D. Rockefeller, Jr., made gifts aggregating many millions to the restoration of Williamsburg and the strengthening of William and Mary—was it able fully to regain the vigor and financial security which the War of the Revolution had so badly impaired.

Books Start Yale

Yale also was created through voluntary generosity and devoted persistence exercised over a preliminary period of fifty-four years before the efforts bore fruit in a charter. In 1647, a lot was set apart for a college in New Haven. The people of that city subscribed £300 at that time, and the people of surrounding communities a like amount. But, due to inability to get sufficient funds, there was delay until 1698, when the matter was revived by the appointment of ten of the principal clergymen of the colony as "trustees to found, erect and govern the college."

These ten met and formed a voluntary society for carrying out the plan. In 1700 they met again, determined to go forward— each giving proof of his willingness to make personal sacrifices by bringing an armful of books from his own library with which to start the library of the college. At that meeting there was a little ceremony, during which each minister stepped forward in his turn and, laying a pile of books on the table, said solemnly: "I give these books for the founding of a college in this colony"— surely a modest start.

The next year a charter was obtained, and for the following fifteen years, under the name of the Collegiate School, the institution existed "somewhere" in Connecticut. No one knew, even at the time, just where, for the students pursued their studies wherever their teachers could be found in their respective homes. For a time it was centered in Killingworth, Connecticut, and then at Saybrook.

In 1718, Elihu Yale—a wealthy resident of London, who had been born in Boston—sent to Cotton Mather, *in response to a letter of request,* several consignments of books and treasures which he had accumulated while Governor of the East India Company. These consignments—except for a portrait of George

I, which the college still possesses—were sold for about £700. The Assembly appropriated land, which was sold for £600, and Bishop Berkeley conveyed his Rhode Island farm of 96 acres. These and other gifts made Yale rich for its day, although Richard G. Boone in his book, *Education in the United States,* estimates that all the gifts to Yale prior to the Revolution totaled no more than $25,000 in cash value.

MANY SMALL BEGINNINGS

Similar stories of meager financial beginnings, and the small but unselfish gifts which brought them into being, might be told of all the other early institutions. For example, Eleazar Wheelock, founder of Dartmouth, once said, "It owns but one tablecloth and that was lately given by a generous lady in Connecticut and of her own manufacture."

Professor Sears thus sums up the financial founding of the pre-Revolutionary War colleges, paying high tribute to the spirit that animated them:

We may say, then, that their beginnings were small; that they were warmly supported by the mother country; that the idea of state support was common, though by no means universal; that there is evidence that no State, with the possible exception of William and Mary, intended to assume full responsibility for the college; that philanthropy clearly did assume that responsibility; and that philanthropy did direct the policy of every college.

We may say that philanthropy was motivated by religion, and that the Church in most cases dominated the movement; that penury was common in all cases; that the thousands of small gifts constituted an important asset in that they popularized the idea of the college and so helped to democratize society; and that the gifts were in the main "to the college" without condition or, if conditioned, they were almost invariably in accord with the essential lines of the school's growth.

Endless evidences of these same arduous struggles in the founding of more recent colleges are to be found in the early annals of nearly all. Mary Lyon, for instance, set out early in the 1830 decade to raise the sum of $30,000, which she felt was necessary to launch the educational institution for women she had in mind.

She traveled hundreds of miles in New England and other eastern states, visited ninety different communities, and obtained 1,800 separate subscriptions—most of them ranging from six cents to one dollar in size and totaling $27,000. Such was the beginning of Mount Holyoke.

Professor William E. Dodd describes the small beginnings of the typical Midwestern colleges as follows:

Peter Cartwright, none too fond of "book-learning" or college preachers, persuaded his people to contribute pitiful sums to the first Methodist college of Illinois; a shilling from one, a day's work from another, and a load of corn or boards from another.

To build Franklin College, in Indiana, children gave pennies, women gave precious calico—long laid away for new dresses—and men delivered bedsteads that could be spared from their homes to the dormitories of the college. Now and then an Easterner—like Abbott Lawrence—sent a fabulous sum to endow some struggling denominational or missionary school, and stamped his name forever upon the map of the country.

MOTIVES OF THE FOUNDERS

What motive lay back of these unselfish, determined endeavors to establish centers of learning in early America? It was, of course, the religious motive. At Harvard, it was stated in these oft-quoted words:

One of the next things we longed for, and looked after, was to advance learning and perpetuate it to Posterity; dreading to leave an illiterate Ministry to the Churches, when our present Ministers shall lie in the Dust.

At William and Mary the founders similarly described their purposes:

That the Church of Virginia may be furnished with a seminary of ministers of the Gospel, and that the youth may be piously educated in good letters and manners and that the Christian faith may be propagated amongst the western Indians, to the glory of Almighty God; to make a place of universal study, or perpetual college of divinity, philosophy, languages and other good arts and sciences.

At Yale:

To found a school "wherein Youth may be instructed in the Arts and Sciences, who through the blessings of Almighty God may be fitted for public employment both in Church and Civil State."

At Columbia:

For Instruction and Education of Youth in the Learned Languages and in the Liberal Arts and Sciences . . . to lead them from the Study of Nature to the Knowledge of Themselves, and of the God of Nature, and their Duty to Him.

There are those who tend to minimize the religious motive back of the founding of our early colleges; but had there been no such motive it seems only fair to conclude that few, if any, would have been established in those rugged days, in the face of such difficulties. It is the love of God and His Kingdom—the brotherhood of men of good will—which surpasses all other loves in its ability to inspire men to unselfish action. Men are not sufficiently moved by love of king or country, of science, of beauty, of knowledge—or by any of the unselfish loyalties except the love of God and humanity—to undertake the appalling burdens involved in founding and maintaining voluntary institutions of higher learning. It is the Church which generates the power to lead men out into these unselfish endeavors. It is religion which is the dynamic energy by which men lift one another out of lethargy, ease, and selfish comfort to devote themselves with impassioned purpose to the service of their fellow men.

As Dr. Donald G. Tewksbury puts it in his book, *The Founding of American Colleges and Universities Before the Civil War*:

The American College was founded to meet the "spiritual necessities" of a new continent. It was designed primarily as a "nursery of ministers," and was fostered as a "child of the Church." The movement for the founding of colleges in America before the Civil War was identified with the rise and growth of religious denominations in this country, and thus it came to partake of the dominant religious character of the formative period of our history and reflect the motives and interests of a religious era.

It is a well-known fact that our Colonial colleges were largely religious in character, but it is not so well understood that, with the exception of a few state universities, practically all the colleges founded between the Revolution and the Civil War were organized, supported and, in most cases, controlled by religious interests. Thus, it may truly be said that the "denominational college" was the prevailing American college of the middle period of our history, as it was of the Colonial period.

DENOMINATIONAL ACTIVITIES

The growth of denominationalism in the nineteenth century and the increase in missionary zeal long kept the churches strongly in the lead in the field of higher education throughout the country. The Congregationalists, the Presbyterians, the Baptists, the Methodists, and the Catholics especially displayed a passion for education which planted colleges on the frontier as it rolled forward across the continent. Before the Civil War religious denominations had established 150 of the 180 permanent colleges and universities in existence in 1860. I say *permanent* because of the appalling number that did not survive. Dr. Tewksbury estimates an 80 per cent mortality among small frontier colleges. Some ambitious regions like Ohio almost literally tried to have a college within *walking* distance of every settlement.

We have already noted the outstanding institutions which the Congregationalists founded. Included in the Presbyterian contribution are Princeton, Hampden-Sydney, Lafayette, Union, Hamilton, Washington and Jefferson, University of Pittsburgh, New York University, Wabash, Davidson, University of Buffalo, and the College of Wooster. Amongst those founded on the initiative of the Baptists are Brown, Colby, Colgate, Bucknell, Denison, Wake Forest, Baylor, Hillsdale, Rochester, Vassar, and Chicago. The Methodists created Randolph-Macon, Wesleyan, Emory, DePauw, Northwestern, Boston, Duke, and Mount Union.

A few of the better known of the 233 colleges maintained by the Catholics are Holy Cross, Fordham, Villanova, Georgetown,

Notre Dame, Loyola, and St. Louis. Episcopalians have to their credit such institutions as William and Mary, Columbia, Trinity, Hobart, and Sewanee, among others. The Quakers—with no less devotion to the cause of education—established Swarthmore, Haverford, Earlham, Guilford, Wilmington, and others. Today, there are approximately 600 colleges still under denominational auspices.

THE QUESTION OF SECULAR CONTROL

Under the leadership of Thomas Jefferson, Thomas Payne, and others of our early political philosophers whose theories of state were derived in part from French Revolutionary thought, there was an endeavor immediately following the Revolution to put all colleges under secular and civic control. Consequently, a few state institutions were founded in the early years of the Republic, among them, in the following order: The University of Georgia, 1785; the University of North Carolina, 1789; the University of Vermont, 1791; and the University of Tennessee in 1794.

During this period there developed considerable feeling, among a minority of the people, against permitting institutions of higher learning to be under the control of the churches, and there was even a determined effort to transfer certain colleges already created by private philanthropy to the ownership and control of the state. This effort was thwarted by the famous Supreme Court decision of Chief Justice Marshall in the Dartmouth case of 1819. This case—argued by Daniel Webster—was a decisive factor in determining whether or not the American people should be definitely free to engage in voluntary undertakings to advance their own culture and well-being. We are still inspired by Webster's moving tribute in this case to his Alma Mater: *"It is a small college, but there are those who love it."*

Chancellor Kent considered this the most important single legal act "to give solidity and inviolability to the literary, religious, charitable and commercial institutions of our country." As a consequence of this slowing up of the founding of state universities, only twenty were established in the United States prior to the Civil War. All of them received fully as much financial help from private philanthropy as the privately established colleges received in grants and subsidies from public treasuries. No hard and fast line had been drawn between the two.

AFTER THE CIVIL WAR

Up to the Civil War, then, private philanthropy under the leadership of the churches had carried almost the entire weight of higher education. In 1862, however, Congress passed the famous Land-Grant Act, signed by President Lincoln. Under its terms the Federal Government offered a grant of land—or scrip to the value thereof—to every state which would, under certain stipulated conditions, undertake the responsibility of creating and maintaining a state college. This combination of federal and state financial aid greatly stimulated the extension of state universities, agricultural colleges, mechanical and industrial institutes, and other institutions of higher and specialized learning. Under the act for state education, 7,830,000 acres have been set aside.

In more recent years many cities have inaugurated municipally supported colleges and universities, or have taken such institutions over from private control—as in the case of the University of Akron, originally Buchtel College. As a consequence of this extension of state and municipal support and a corresponding subsidence of Protestant denominational support, taxation is now assuming a larger proportion of the load of higher education. Philanthropy, however, still carries the heavy share of the burden. The sum total of private benefactions to higher education in 1950—according to the most accurate statistics available—was over $320,000,000, the largest total of voluntary giving to education ever recorded at that time. This is surely a significant fact.

Reference was made above to a decline of Protestant denominational support for higher education. Catholic support for education, however, far from declining, is definitely increasing. The Catholic Church in America owns and operates 424 seminaries, 233 colleges and universities, 2,441 high schools, and 8,889 elementary schools, according to the 1952 official *Catholic Directory* (published by P. J. Kennedy and Sons, New York). The students enrolled in these 11,987 Catholic privately supported educational institutions in 1952 numbered 3,571,272, as compared to a total student enrollment in 1951 of 3,456,187 in 11,767 schools. This increase was made in spite of the general decline of 7 per cent in college enrollments throughout the United States.

SOURCES OF STRENGTH

There is a touching affection for the private college on the part of many people, friends as well as alumni. With it goes a continued willingness to pour out voluntary gifts in such volume as to make it unlikely that state universities in America will ever displace the independent college. There is ample room—and need—for both. The deep-seated loyalty which independent colleges have inspired is in considerable part accounted for by the sacrifices and unselfish devotion which their founding and maintenance have evoked from each succeeding generation. The extent of these sacrifices and the quality of this devotion have been suggested in some of the preceding passages.

Our freedom-loving Republic and our independent college were fashioned together—at the same time, by the same people, after the same pattern, and in the same intensity of devotion to the same high cause. By some curious alchemy our forefathers transmitted to these schools a tensile strength which has rendered them all but indestructible.

During the past quarter century many supposedly sturdy institutions collapsed. Banks by the thousands perished in the 1930 holocaust, businesses by the hundreds of thousands failed, and the bonds of thousands of taxing units defaulted; but not a dozen accredited private colleges of senior grade failed to survive. Dr. Robert L. Kelly, secretary emeritus of the Association of American Colleges, suggests: "If you have any doubt of the vitality of the private American college, just try to kill one!"

The liberal arts college—founded and sustained by private philanthropy—sends its roots down more deeply into American tradition and affection than any other of our institutions. A few of them, of course, have not been well located or firmly founded, and may not survive. But the institution itself will probably endure in America as long as our present form of government

endures. For it represents the very spirit of free Americans—
the spirit of unselfish men who have voluntarily created centers
of learning for eager and ambitious American youth. Our private
college and our democracy, spun from the same strands, are
firmly interwoven in the fabric of our society. They are the
closest of friends, and one can scarcely conceive that either will
ever abandon the other.

CHAPTER IV

Philanthropy and the Hospitals

O F ALL the great institutions which philanthropy has helped
to develop in the service of American civilization, the hospital is one of the most useful and appealing—and, at the same
time, one of the most inarticulate. It has not by any means been
as effective as it deserved to be in interpreting its story, its work,
and its value to the American people.

EARLY BEGINNINGS IN AMERICA

A few small early hospitals were established along the eastern
coast; the first was perhaps one built by the East India Company on Manhattan Island in 1663 to care for the Company's
Negroes and for ill soldiers. Other similar temporary hospitals
—pesthouses would be a better name—were established for
sailors with contagious diseases. But none of these hospitals developed into anything permanent.

The hospital which has been in continuous existence the
longest in this country is probably Old Blockley, established in
1731, originally the sick ward for the Alms House at Philadelphia. This was not a hospital open to the general public, but
was simply for the use of those wards of the city who needed
medical attention—often, it is likely, because of an excess of
indulgence in India rum. Old Blockley was the progenitor of
the present Philadelphia City Hospital.

The second oldest existing hospital may be said to be Bellevue
in New York City, which—like Old Blockley—was not originally
open to the general public, but was established in 1736 as the
"Publick Workhouse and House of Correction of the City of
New York." In the early days it was, thus, a combined penal and
health institution. The magnificent center of health which grew
from this early beginning is, of course, owned by the City of New

42

York and is tax-supported, but still attracts generous philanthropic aid.

The earliest general hospital established in the United States —still surviving—is Charity Hospital at New Orleans. It was founded in 1737 by a gift of $2,500 from Jean Louis, a sailor and later an officer in the East India Company. It was called St. John Hospital for forty years. After being demolished by a storm, it was rebuilt by further private gifts and renamed Charity Hospital. Although it is now owned by the state, it is a continued object of private support. In its group of buildings are several memorial units—the Richard Milliken Memorial Hospital for Children, the Delgado Memorial, the Hutchinson Nurses' Home, and the John Dibert Tuberculosis Hospital. This situation well illustrates the close partnership between voluntary philanthropy and tax appropriation which has so effectively aided in building up the nation's magnificent equipment for fighting disease.

The first general hospital in the East open to citizens not detained against their will was established in Philadelphia. It is in existence today under the same name with which it started its career in 1751—Pennsylvania Hospital. It was founded by two doctors: a medical doctor, Thomas Bond, and a famous doctor of humanity whose name can never be lightly passed over in any discussion of philanthropy's role in America, Dr. Benjamin Franklin.

This great citizen, undertaking to raise funds for a hospital, started one of his perennial subscription lists in 1750. He obtained some voluntary pledges but not to the amount necessary; so, in 1751, he petitioned the Provincial Assembly both for a charter and for "pecuniary aid." Certain rural members of the Assembly held back their approval since they saw no advantage to themselves in a city hospital. Franklin—as adept at winning votes as at coaxing contributions—suggested that the Assembly make a grant of £2,000 on condition that the citizens of Philadelphia make a voluntary contribution of like amount. The rural members, sure that the merchants of the city would be unwilling to make such a gift, approved the grant. With this as a lever, Franklin then quickly persuaded the citizens of Philadelphia to subscribe their portion of the fund. It was an early instance of the effectiveness of a "conditional offer."

Pennsylvania Hospital was opened in 1755—its corporate seal bearing the inscription *"Take care of him, and I will repay thee."* It has been serving the citizens of that community ever since. Its progress has been made possible by continuous teamwork between the legislature and private philanthropy. The citizens would raise a fund by subscription and the legislature would make another grant; then the citizens would start another subscription and the legislature would appropriate more funds—between the two, the institution has grown and prospered. Its assets now total over five million dollars, and it is still under the control of a voluntary board of trustees.

In New York, also, private philanthropy took the initiative in founding the city's first general hospital—New York Hospital, established in 1770 by private subscription. From the beginning it, too, received help in the form of a grant from the Municipal Assembly—and, a few years later, an annual grant from the State of New York. Considerable help was further solicited and obtained in England. It is now owned jointly by the Society of the New York Hospital and Cornell University. A few years ago it received a bequest from the estate of Payne Whitney which ranks as one of the largest individual gifts ever made to a hospital.

The oldest hospital in New England is the Boston Dispensary, initiated in 1796 by the Reverend Samuel Parker and his associates. Their purpose was not so much to found an institution as to "give medical advice and relief to the sick poor." Incorporated in 1801, it has been in continuous existence ever since. In 1837, a certain Dr. Oliver Wendell Holmes wrote the managers a brief note, requesting consideration for appointment to a vacancy in the medical department. It was granted. The Boston Dispensary is still owned and controlled by a voluntary board of managers and has been the beneficiary of many generous gifts and bequests through all its years.

The oldest general hospital in Boston, *Massachusettes General Hospital*, was also founded by private initiative, but with the added help of legislative appropriations. In 1804, a bequest of

$5,000 was received from William Phillips for the founding of a hospital. After other gifts were made and a substantial fund accumulated, the state legislature offered property for the institution—*if* $100,000 should be obtained by private subscription for the cost of construction. This challenge was hopefully met, and the institution was opened in 1818. Within the first twenty years of its life over $600,000 was given or bequeathed to the Massachusetts General Hospital in large individual amounts. In 1827 it received a gift of $100,000 from John McLean, and a few years later John Redman gave another $100,000. This scale of giving was most unusual a hundred year ago. An institution which was able to attract such gifts in those days must have early proved itself indispensable.

SOME SUMMARY FACTS

Today, there are 6,430 registered hospitals in the United States, which may be classified in three general groups: those owned by city, county, state, or Federal Government, and supported by taxation; those owned by voluntary groups of public-spirited citizens and supported by philanthropy, either private, religious, or fraternal; and proprietary hospitals operated by individual doctors or groups of doctors in connection with their private practice, or owned by corporations for the use of their own employees.

The *tax-supported hospitals*—other than those of the Army, Navy, Public Health Administration, and Veterans Administration—are maintained by local or regional units of government for necessary medical services to the poor, or to other wards of society. Over two thirds of their work is for those afflicted by mental and nervous diseases. They have some general beds, but these are only about one fifth of their total.

The *voluntary hospital*—supported by private philanthropy —carries most of the burden of hospitalization for the general public. It is to such an institution that the average citizen goes who is not obliged to be a ward of the community. Most of the beds of voluntary hospitals are for general purposes, and philanthropy treats over twice the number of general patients cared for in tax-supported hospitals.

The *proprietary hospitals* are mainly to be found in smaller communities where there is not sufficient public leadership or numerical demand and support to establish community hospitals of a voluntary character.

The American Medical Association made a census of hospitals in 1950, and the following data are taken from its report in the *Journal* of the Association, dated May 21, 1951:

There are 6,530 registered hospitals in the United States—with 1,-456,000 beds. Their annual admissions are 17,023,000. 1,912 of these hospitals are tax-supported; 3,169 are voluntary philanthropic institutions, of which 1,097 are operated by Church bodies; 1,449 are proprietary institutions.

PHILANTHROPY'S SHARE IS LARGE

Philanthropy has not found it insuperably difficult to provide funds to build and equip the 3,169 hospitals which it has established for the general public. The usual devices for raising money which have been current in succeeding generations have been employed by the hospital. The early institutions were built by subscription lists and expanded by bequests. In the latter half of the nineteenth century many were founded on the initiative of church groups and women's clubs—the required resources being raised by an evocation of community good will surpassing any united effort that our people had ever made in behalf of a voluntary enterprise.

In line with its confident policy of appealing for voluntary gifts, the hospital was the first philanthropic institution to copy from the Y.M.C.A. the modern campaign methods described in Chapter X. Long before college, chureh, or welfare society realized the value of the intensive campaign, the hospital had adopted it. In fact, some of the early spectacular "drives" in behalf of hospitals were staged several years before World War I. Recently, the organized campaign has been almost the only fund-raising technique used by hospitals—except for those fortunate few which have received individual bequests sufficient for their needs.

THE RELIGIOUS MOTIVE

As with so many other philanthropic institutions, much of the drive back of the building of our voluntary hospitals has been the religious motive. "Heal the sick" is an injunction which has spurred Catholics to establish well over 800 hospitals, and Protestants to take the initiative in establishing many of our other voluntary institutions. The Jews have also been moved by the traditional passion of their religion to establish more than forty hospitals.

The hospital has a longer history than any other of our social institutions, and we have already noted how zealously the Christian Church founded and maintained hospitals from the earliest centuries after Christ. There is a great present-day hospital in Paris—the *Hôtel Dieu*—which was one of the early Christian institutions of healing, having been founded A.D. 660. All through the Christian era there has been no form of humanitarian service more popular among Church people than the hospital.

THE PROBLEM OF MAINTENANCE

Although it has not been too difficult for public-spirited men and women to build our voluntary hospitals, the task of operating them has frequently proved almost too much. The problem of operation has not yet been satisfactorily solved, although there is a plan now in use, group hospitalization, which holds out hope that current operating costs can perhaps be met with somewhat less anxiety in the years ahead.

The basic reason for the operating problem lies in the difficulty of finding a scale of charges which will be equitable for all classes of potential patients. If the scale is put too high, the middle classes will not make use of the facilities as fully as they should, and at any given time too many beds will be idle. If too low, the income will prove less than the actual cost of operation, even though the average occupancy remains high. *Practically no voluntary hospital in the country operates without an annual deficit.* Consequently, most of them have had to make annual appeals to meet current operating deficits, and the returns from these repeated appeals have too often proved disappointing to the institutions and wearying to their friends. The new plan of group hospitalization is proving helpful. There are now 80,000,000 persons in America enrolled in these private and voluntary group hospitalization and medical plans—the Blue Cross and others. It is estimated that before long the total will reach 90,000,000.

PRESIDENT'S COMMISSION ON THE HEALTH NEEDS OF THE NATION

During his second administration President Truman urged upon Congress a compulsory health insurance plan which would have involved large federal appropriations and considerable federal control. Members of the American Medical Association and many others opposed the plan vigorously on the grounds of governmental encroachment on individual freedom, and the bill was not passed.

President Truman then appointed the President's Commission on the Health Needs of the Nation to study the problem. Late in 1952 this commission brought in a report which advocated a comprehensive program which calls upon federal, state, and local governments, physicians, and private citizens to join forces in support of better health for all citizens. The basis of this proposed program is prepaid health service, privately financed, with a health authority in each state, and with the Federal Government encouraging the total operation by a system of insurance. It is not yet clear how this proposal will be received by the public and by Congress.

The best estimate of the current operating costs of our voluntary hospitals places the total at about $220,000,000 per year. The sources of this annual income vary widely. Some institutions have substantial endowments, while others have practically none. In the national total the income is estimated about as follows: 64 per cent from patients, 20 per cent from endowments, 10 per cent from voluntary gifts, 5 per cent from city or county for special services, 1 per cent from miscellaneous sources.

The amount of money necessary to maintain voluntary hospitals—the ones most generally used by the rank and file of our citizenry—might seem burdensome if considered by itself, but when compared with some other figures it seems ridiculously small. The President's Committee on the Cost of Medical Care points out that the American people pay in a single year $360,-000,000 for patent medicines and $125,000,000 to quacks, cultists, and irregular practitioners. These two expenditures combined indicate that we throw away in vain and illusory attempts to gain health over twice as much as the entire cost of operating all the voluntary hospitals in every state of the Union.

Once again, Dr. Haven Emerson reminds us that sickness and accidents cost the American people an average of $30 apiece each year; whereas our entire bill for independent hospitals costs only an average of $2 per person. Obviously, it would be plain economy to pay more into our hospitals rather than less. If we would use them more fully, and provide more funds for their thoroughly effective operation, such expenditures would lift many times their costs from the present heavy burden of quackery, unnecessary ill health, and decreased physical efficiency under which the people of the nation—well equipped as it is—are still suffering.

Speaking at the Waldorf-Astoria Hotel in November, 1952, at a dinner marking the centennial of Mount Sinai Hospital, Governor Thomas E. Dewey declared that what had made American hospitals great also had brought amazing results in countless fields of endeavor. "In this whole death struggle between totalitarianism and freedom," he said, "the secret weapon of America—far more than the atom bomb or the hydrogen bomb—is our freedom."

Governor Dewey said he saw no conflict between the free enterprise system and the existence of government hospitals to meet special needs. Most of these hospitals are necessary, he added, "but that is only half of the answer. The rest of the answer is that none of them would be any good unless the dominant quality of American hospital service was that established by the voluntary hospitals—the sense of social responsibility, if you will, the sense of charity—the knowledge that I am indeed my brother's keeper. It is the voluntary hospitals that set the standards. It is the free medical profession that keeps breaking through supersonic barriers and then makes new achievements available to all the people."

CHAPTER V

Voluntary Philanthropy Pioneers Social Progress

THE title of this chapter states, in the fewest possible words, the central thesis of this book. Philanthropy's role through the centuries—most of all through the last two thousand years —has been that of a beneficent and courageous pathfinder. Armed with the Biblical "Faith, Hope, and Charity, these three," men and women of good will and good sense, working together of their own volition, have unselfishly created and maintained countless instrumentalities for the betterment of human life.

In the preceding chapters we have tried to define philanthropy, look into its motives, and describe the development of two of its greatest achievements—the college and the hospital. We have emphasized the inspiring role of religion, especially the practical activities of the organized Christian Church.

Here I want to try once more to show *why* and *how* free-will, self-directed philanthropy has filled its unique role, and to take a bird's-eye view of the many fields into which it has entered. Perhaps we shall then see more fully the debt that our Western civilization owes to co-operative good will. Also, on the other side, the tragedy we should be inviting if changes in the pattern of our national life were to lessen the spontaneous springs of unselfish giving.

For three hundred years voluntary philanthropy has been the constant, quiet leader in our nation's progress toward higher levels of well-being. Almost every cultural advance has been pioneered by private associations of persons willing to put their personal means at the service of a social cause. After the usefulness of such a cause has thus been demonstrated, the electorate has often adopted it into the family of tax-supported enterprises. Thus, philanthropy has been a sort of John the Baptist in our democratic progress, preparing the way, modestly willing to "decrease" in prestige if only the cause shall "increase." A few illustrations of the historic interplay between philanthropy and government in the evolution of our present cultural and social agencies may prove of interest.

FREE PUBLIC EDUCATION

Free public education, for instance, is now regarded as the inalienable right of every child, and we of this generation accept the public school as an integral, matter-of-fact part of our governmental system. But for two centuries the public school in America was a "charity" in most sections of the country, outside of New England, maintained wholly or in part by the voluntary efforts of religious and philanthropic societies. It would be difficult to find a sane person today who would argue that public schools should not be institutions of government—but, in 1671, the Governor of Virginia is reported to have exclaimed: "I thank God there are no free schools nor printing presses in Virginia and I hope we shall not have them these hundred years." And in the early part of the nineteenth century a member of the Indiana General Assembly closed his impassioned oration against free public schools with these words: "When I die I want my epitaph written—*Here lies an enemy of free schools.*"

In addition to the lead which philanthropy took in founding and maintaining public schools, it organized educational societies as propagandizing agencies to urge state legislatures to assume their rightful responsibility. Thus, in the course of years, philanthropy was able to persuade government to take over by degrees the major part of this social responsibility which it had shouldered voluntarily in the service of the people at a time when no one else would carry it forward.

LIBRARIES

Our free public libraries were similarly created and maintained by voluntary contributions for many years before being adopted by government. Someone has said that "civilization expands its most benignant and effective agencies of progress only under protest." The imaginative minority has a task convincing the ma-

jority. We protested long and vigorously against voting support
to libraries, but because philanthropy patiently led the way
we have today something like 11,000 free public libraries, with
162,000,000 volumes on their shelves, which circulate 340,000,000
books a year to 20,000,000 borrowers. The major part of the
cost of operating these libraries now comes from tax funds.

Benjamin Franklin and his associates created the first library,
in 1731, in Philadelphia; other philanthropists gave voluntary
funds to establish libraries in Charleston, Providence, New York
City, Baltimore, and elsewhere. It was not until 117 years later
that the first state—Massachusetts—passed an act *permitting* a
municipality to tax itself for the support of a library. Even with
this permissive act, the citizens of our most enlightened communities were slow to vote funds, and the free library long continued to be regarded as a luxury. The son of a president of
Harvard, for example, published a book in 1875 in which he
endeavored to dissuade his fellow citizens against a certain ap-
propriation for a library. He asks: "Upon what principle can a
citizen who has the power to cast his ballot justify himself in
voting increased taxation upon his neighbor for the purpose of
establishing a library?"

Philanthropy gave 150 years to the patient demonstration of
the social value of public libraries before the general citizenry
was ready to vote any considerable tax appropriations toward
their support. And it might still be providing the major support
had it not been for the canny generosity of Andrew Carnegie,
who began to offer handsome library buildings to thousands of
cities on condition that they would thereafter support the institution.

It was this offer of something for nothing which suddenly
turned the scale of public opinion in many a city. In Edinburgh,
Scotland, for instance, the voters were induced to reject a proposal to establish a public library there by the display of sand-
wich signs with the following inscription:

Ratepayers!
Resist this Free Library Dodge
and Save Yourselves from the Burden of £6,000
of Additional Taxation!

But only five years later—when Andrew Carnegie offered a free gift of £50,000 to erect a library building—the Edinburgh voters accepted it readily enough, and the library was established.

Mr. Carnegie's similar strategy in America had the same effect. It speeded up the acceptance of the public library as a proper object of tax support. Dr. Faunce, late president of Brown, wrote at the beginning of the twentieth century: "Libraries have spread from sea to sea by a happy contagion. They have become a noble American epidemic." Although the typical American library today is a member of the tax-supported family, it still enjoys considerable support from voluntary philanthropy also, some of our great libraries now being interesting hybrids—the fruit of taxation, private endowment, and voluntary philanthropy. The great New York Public Library, for instance, is supported by the Samuel Tilden, John Jacob Astor, and Lenox endowments, by tax appropriations, and by voluntary gifts.

PIONEERING—A "MINORITY MOVEMENT"

A voluntary philanthropy might be described as a minority movement which cannot yet obtain a majority vote of taxpayers and voters, but which is nevertheless carried forward by an optimistic group of persons willing to give their money and energy to a good cause in which they believe. When it becomes so popular—or its need becomes so evident—that it develops a majority following, then government, local, state, or federal, adopts it. The late Felix M. Warburg said: "The feeling was, and I think rightly, that experiments should be made by private institutions before the public's funds were risked in large amounts on schemes which have not been tried out thoroughly as yet. . . . I am quite sure the method has saved the United States a very large amount of money." This viewpoint is strongly held by the great philanthropic foundations.

Voluntary philanthropy is constantly pioneering in new fields. For example, *preventive and educational health work* outside of hospitals—such as the work of visiting nurses; dental clinics; anti-tuberculosis, cancer, and leprosy campaigns; the work of the Red Cross; and so on—has been pioneered almost exclusively by private philanthropy, and much of it is still carried on in this way.

One might go on in the recital of an astonishing number of present-day institutions that are now the accepted responsibility of government, but which were created by independent efforts. There are, for illustration, our *reformatories*, which we regard as an essential part of our penal system. Yet only a century ago it was not thought that the state owed any special consideration to youthful offenders. Consequently, our first reformatory was founded in 1820 in New York through the personal activity of Edward Livingston and others. Leaders in other cities followed the example of New York, and a generation later, in 1848, the first tax-supported reformatory was established at Westboro, Massachusetts. Until voluntary institutions made a clear demonstration the voters had no vision of the human wastage that might be lessened by separating wayward children from hardened criminals.

One instinctively thinks of the Washington Monument as a proud possession of the people of the United States—but even *it* was initiated by voluntary philanthropy, after thirty-four years of effort to persuade the government to do so had ended in controversy and failure. It is hard for us to understand how political prejudice against the father of our country was ever powerful enough to prevent the passage of a congressional act for memorializing him—but it was.

Private individuals had to take the initiative. In 1833, the Washington National Monument Society—organized as a philanthropic endeavor—proceeded to collect the million dollars thought necessary to erect a worthy monument. By 1847 the Society had gathered $70,000, the cornerstone was laid, and, in a few years time, the monument was 152 feet high—where it paused for a quarter of a century. Then, fifty years after the Society started its work and eighty-five years after the death of Washington, the Federal Government finally made an appropriation sufficient to complete the monument. The total cost was approximately $1,000,000, of which $300,000 was contributed by individual donors. To this day, the observer may see the different coloration of the stones, above and below the 152-foot level, where private contributions halted and federal appropriations took over.

Voluntary philanthropy has rendered numerous other notable services to the nation in sponsoring *moral and social reforms*—such as the drive against slavery—which have later been incor-

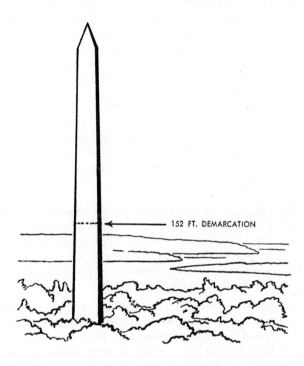

152 FT. DEMARCATION

porated in the law of the land. It was government which actually ended human slavery in the nineteenth century in British, French, Portuguese, and Dutch possessions, as well as in America, but it was the dauntless devotion of organized groups of private citizens to this great humanitarian cause which made legislative action possible.

We might cite many other examples of important social and cultural developments which have slowly grown out of initial efforts by socially minded individuals. Indeed, almost the only institutions in our whole philanthropic enterprise that have not been, in some measure, incorporated into the official structure of government are the churches and other religious and character-building agencies. By a queer twist of democratic procedure, this group of institutions here evolved in precisely the opposite direction—for churches started out in the New England theocratic colonies as functions of government.

With the exception of these religious agencies, it would seem to be the pattern of American experience for voluntary philanthropy to pioneer the way for new cultural and social endeavors, and then for government to absorb a portion of such attempts into its tax-supported program of service to its people. How far this process should go, and how much "responsibility" government should assume in matters formerly considered the moral responsibility of the individual or the family, is one of the fundamental questions now facing the American people.

THE AMERICAN WAY

It is generally agreed that the distinctive character of our nation is that of a *land of opportunity*, not of guaranteed rewards —a land where a high premium is placed on initiative, individual effort, and moral qualities. In the words of American Viewpoint, Inc., an educational membership corporation, which have bearing on the subject under discussion:

Progress comes not through coercion but through voluntary co-operation of self-directing individuals seeking to build a better world for themselves and for their neighbors. . . . Here then is the essential doctrine of individualism upon which Western civilization has been built. It grew out of the Christian teaching of the worth of human personality and the possibility of achieving an ideal order by human effort and co-operation. . . . This is individualism as opposed to collectivism . . . the American viewpoint.

Looking to government—which means ever-greater compulsory taxation—has not been the American Way.

As government has gradually taken over the load, or a portion of the load, of the many agencies which voluntary efforts pioneered, *philanthropy's scope has not decreased.* By any strictly mathematical formula it should have been lessened by just the amount that government assumed. But simple plus-and-minus arithmetic gives no true measure of American spirit and achievement.

Strangely enough, every expansion of government in these fields has been accompanied by a similar expansion of philanthropy in the same, or in new, fields. We have seen how the Land-Grant Act in President Lincoln's administration brought into being the modern tax-supported state university in the 1860's. Over two hundred state institutions of higher education have since been established. Did this lessen philanthropy's interest in higher education? On the contrary, voluntary gifts to private colleges and universities in recent days have sometimes totaled as much *in one year* as they totaled *in all the two hundred years* of collegiate history prior to that act. During the year 1870 the total private gifts to education in America equaled $8,593,740; during the year 1950 they exceeded $300,000,000.

The whole scope and volume of voluntary activities has steadily expanded as government has increased its range of social interests. One can no more set a limit to voluntary giving than he can set a limit to the spirit of man. Vast areas of finer living remain to be explored. Philanthropy is our pioneer—our advance scout. It goes on ahead, unhampered by governmental inhibitions and rigidities, spying out new fields for the occupation of our ever-advancing civilization.

As long as such fields beckon to the race, philanthropy will go on and on—always on the march, always ahead of official government. And when, as in the case of public schools and antislavery, government finally moves up to the positions which philanthropy had taken, philanthropy gladly takes up new humanitarian quests, devoting increased energy and enthusiasm to the exploring of new fields of effort. Philanthropy has the long view.

Today a vast work lies ahead—a work which those who love America must not neglect in the mistaken notion that "there's no longer any need for private philanthropy." With all our boasted progress in the development of mechanisms, gadgets, and comforts, we can boast little enough of our progress in good manners, in moral character, in the capacity to dwell together in unselfish good will, in the true appreciation of cultural and spiritual values. America still challenges independent spirits with great unfinished tasks. The day of the pioneer has not passed.

CHAPTER VI

Other Fruits of American Philanthropy

ATTENTION has now been drawn to philanthropy's role as a hopeful pioneer of social progress. Half a dozen illustrations were given as examples of the process by which public auspices so often take over projects initiated by private effort. This pioneering role is much like that of experimentation or "research" in such fields as guidance, natural science, or industry —a policy to which America has become completely committed. Social, educational, and medical pioneering has also had its Edisons, its Millikans, and its Ketterings.

And the results—the by-products, the fruits, the trophies— have been equally numerous. The complete list, were it possible to draw it up, would come close to covering the important humanitarian institutions and services of our land. Some of them will come as a surprise to almost any reader, because he has known them only as public institutions—and taken them for granted at that.

Without trying to be exhaustive, here is an alphabetical list of the more influential movements or institutions that owe their origin to the initiative and the persistence of private philanthropy:

SOME INFLUENTIAL AMERICAN INSTITUTIONS WHOSE
ORIGINS STEM FROM VOLUNTARY PHILANTHROPY

Adult Education	Girl Scouts, C.Y.O., Y.M.H.A.,
Aged, Homes for the	etc.
Arbitration	Churches
Art, Christian	Colleges
Babies, Shelters for	Cultural Movements
Cathedrals	Evening Schools
Character-Building Agencies:	Fire Departments (Town & City)
Y.M.C.A., Y.W.C.A., Boy Scouts,	Free (Public) Education

Health Agencies
Hospitals
Humanitarian Care
Industrial Training
International Friendship
Kindergartens
Lepers, Care of
Libraries, Free Public
Memorial Monuments
Mental Hygiene
Missionary Enterprises
Moral Education
Museums
Negro Race, Help and Schools for
Orphanages
Peace, World
Pensions for the Aged
Prison Reform

Reading Circles
Recreational Facilities
Reformatories
Scholarships, Fellowships
Schools for the Deaf and Dumb,
    Blind, Feeble-Minded, Handi-
    capped
Salvation Army
Slavery, Abolition of
Social Security
Social Settlements
Social Welfare Movements
Southern Mountain Schools
Summer Schools
Sunday Schools
Vocational Guidance
Washington Monument
Women, Education of

Imposing or surprising as the above list may appear, the best way to understand the actual workings of the voluntary spirit is to trace the evolution of the better-known movements. This will reveal the creative influence of individual leaders, the amazing quality of co-operation that characterizes Americans, and the variety of fields into which the resulting efforts have led the way. Colleges and hospitals have already been treated at length, and other activities mentioned. The reader will pardon some repetition necessary to the convenient grouping of evidence.

NORMAL SCHOOLS

Schools to train teachers—normal schools we called them, now primarily the function of the state systems of education—grew out of voluntary efforts first initiated in 1805 by Professor S. R. Hall at Concord, New Hampshire. Then, in 1839, Edward Dwight of Massachusetts offered $10,000 toward the establishment of the Massachusetts Normal School, provided the state would give a like amount. Under the stimulus of this offer the state appropriated tax funds, and three normal school were soon opened.

INDUSTRIAL EDUCATION

Industrial training was also started by private efforts. The first institution of the sort was Rensselaer Polytechnic, established at Troy, New York, in 1824. Other manual labor schools of a voluntary nature were soon established and "the function of intelligent labor was magnified." Out of these manual labor seminaries grew a variety of "vocational" schools and also modern technical schools of science, engineering, design, architecture, art, and so on, which now occupy so large a place in the curricula of both private and state-supported institutions of higher education. This is one of America's great achievements, and one of the sources of her strength.

SCHOOLS FOR THE DEAF

In 1817, private benevolence initiated the first organized work in this country for the education of the deaf. The Reverend T. H. Gallaudet founded the Connecticut Asylum for the Education of Deaf and Dumb Persons. Personal gifts provided most of the funds, although the state legislature was induced to appropriate $5,000. Later Congress gave 23,000 acres of land and the name was changed to the American Asylum for the Deaf. This personal pioneering by Dr. Gallaudet was fruitful. By 1880 there were 61 institutions, with 8,000 members. More than half of them were tax-supported and a number of the privately financed institutions also received some state or municipal aid.

One college for the deaf—Gallaudet College, at Washington, D. C.—was founded in 1857 on the private initiative of the philanthropist Amos Kendall, although the United States Government was soon induced to come to its support.

At present one of the greatest of these schools is the privately endowed Clark School for the Deaf, at Northampton, Massachusetts. It was here that the young Grace Goodhue was a teacher before her marriage to the late Calvin Coolidge. In 1927 the friends of President and Mrs. Coolidge honored them by making voluntary contributions of $3,000,000 to the endowment of the school as a Coolidge Memorial Fund.

THE WAR AGAINST BLINDNESS

Our first three schools for the blind were founded and maintained by private efforts. In 1832 Dr. S. G. Howe, valiant young crusader of Boston, established there the Perkins Institute, the first educational institution in American for the blind. Two similar institutions were founded shortly thereafter, one in New York and one in Philadelphia.

State legislatures were gradually persuaded to take up this appealing educational work, although to this day much of the most significant service to the blind is being done through workshops and schools maintained in scores of cities by private organizations. Leadership in the increasing service to the blind is being given by philanthropic agencies—notably the National Society for the Prevention of Blindness and the American Foundation for the Blind. Both these agencies obtain from voluntary gifts the financial support for their constructive program of research and co-ordination.

MENTAL HYGIENE

Schools for the feeble-minded were also initiated by private philanthropy in the middle of the nineteenth century by the same Dr. Howe—husband of Julia Ward Howe, author of the "Battle Hymn of The Republic" who opened the first school for the blind. Always ready to break a lance in any pioneering service for humanity, Dr. Howe early recognized that some of his blind pupils were also subnormal mentally. He opened an experimental school for the feeble-minded at Barre, Massachusetts. The results were so convincing that within a few years New York established a state institution for the feeble-minded. The fruitage of his careful experimentation came quickly. This specialized education has now become largely a state function, although there are a few voluntary institutions still operating in the field. The school established by Dr. Howe was also the forerunner of modern developments in the general fields of psychiatry and mental hygiene.

EVENING SCHOOLS

Another educational project destined to have wide influence was the launching of evening schools in 1834 by the Public School Society of New York City, a voluntary philanthropic organization. This first evening school was primarily an endeavor to combat vagrancy and truancy among children. Within two years the Society had fifteen evening schools, with 8,000 pupils. Following this success in New York, similar public-spirited organizations introduced the evening school into Boston, carrying it forward under private auspices until it was incorporated into the public school system in 1857.

One's most extravagant appraisal of the contribution which this new educational idea has made to the well-being of America can scarcely overreach the actual facts. Until private philanthropy pioneered the night school, formal classroom study was thought of as a daytime occupation only; but from that time on, it also became the privilege of those who must work by day—young and old alike. The stimulus which organized evening schools gave to the enlargement of the mental horizon of persons beyond school age has gathered momentum from that day to this, bearing fruit in the most varied phases of adult education—now a national concern.

In 1857 Peter Cooper, one of New York's greatest philanthropists and an officer of the Public School Society, adopted the evening school idea on the level of higher education and founded Cooper Union as an institute for technical instruction in the arts and trades. The example of his school was eventually followed in all the other great cities of the land—fostered by municipality, state, and private philanthropy alike.

SCHOLARSHIPS

This constant desire to bring specialized educational opportunities within the grasp of eager youth specially fitted to make good use of them is one of the most characteristic aspects of philanthropy in America. Not only has it been a leading factor in the founding of countless schools and colleges, but it continues in the scholarship or fellowship which is so prominent a feature

of our educational policy. It is another striking evidence that
the individual is at the center of our thought. A scholarship is
an individual award. It provides greater opportunity for growth
and service by an individual boy or girl, man or woman. This
personal nature—both in the giving and in the receiving—gives
the scholarship its strong appeal.

Accompanying a recent alumni magazine article acknowledg-
ing current alumni gifts for scholarships, there appeared a delightful photograph of two students standing in front of the
college chapel. Across the face of the picture was written: "You
have helped make it possible for us to continue here. Thanks!"

From earliest days our schools did everything possible to help
ambitious and deserving boys and girls to get an education.
"Labor and Learning"—the motto on an early college seal—was
the policy everywhere. Scholars were expected to render their
best service to the school, in grateful acknowledgement of what
the school was giving them.

The first conspicuous international use of scholarships came
after the Boxer Rebellion in China. Instead of taking the in-
demnity owed us in cash, the United States asked China to spend
the entire sum on scholarships for picked Chinese students to be
sent to America for study here. This concept of exchange students in both directions—made possible by both public and private grants—has for years been promoted by the Institute of
International Education, and by individual institutions. Perhaps
no philanthropic activity has paid better dividends.

Scholarship opportunities in our schools and colleges were
never greater. As the late Horace Taft, founder of Taft School,
put it: "We are always looking for pace-setters—boys who will
help us keep our standards high." A recent page of one metropolitan newspaper carried eight stories of scholarship awards.
A former educational editor of the *New York Herald Tribune*
said not long ago that he believed any boy of real ability and
determination could secure a scholarship, if he really desired
it, in one of the good preparatory schools. Philanthropy is constantly alive in this field, helping deserving individuals to help
themselves. And now the Federal Government has done a magnificent job in providing tax-supported scholarships (G.I. benefits) for veterans of World War II and the Korean War.

KINDERGARTENS

In 1859 another specialized field of education at the opposite end of the scale—the kindergarten—was opened up by private initiative. It was first organized as a charity kindergarten for poor and uncared-for waifs, but was soon discovered to be an excellent form of preschool training for normal children.

The first such kindergartens in American were opened in the 1850 decade by German immigrants who had been associated with Friedrich Froebel in Blankenburg, Germany: Louisa Frankenberg in Columbus, Ohio; and the wife of Carl Schurz—who had been impelled to come to the United States in 1852, in Watertown, Wisconsin. An English-speaking kindergarten was opened in Boston in 1860 by Elizabeth P. Peabody, the sister of Horace Mann. After their merit was proved by private philanthropists the public school system began to adopt them—first in St. Louis, where Carl Schurz had settled after the Civil War. Then in the 1880's—a quarter century after the pioneering in America had begun—three states, Connecticut, Indiana, and Illinois, enacted laws which permitted the use of public school funds for the education of children of kindergarten age. By 1900 there were over 5,000 kindergartens in the United States —3,000 of them being a part of the public schools system, 1,300 still conducted as private institutions, and 800 supported by charity.

MUSEUMS

This important and interesting technique of mass education and entertainment—the Museum—was also instituted in America by private initiative. Among early examples were the Museum and Art Gallery of the New York Historical Society, founded in 1804; the Pennsylvania Academy of Fine Arts, in 1805; the Boston Athenaeum, in 1807; the Yale School of Fine Arts, in 1825; the National Academy of Design, in 1826—all of which were given by private philanthropy for the use of the people. Later on, municipalities, states, and the Federal Government developed a great variety of museums and voted tax funds for their support, but the people's appreciation of these storehouses of historical, scientific, and artistic treasures had been cultivated through countless gifts made by persons of culture and public spirit.

The greatest museum in America—the *Smithsonian Institution* in Washington, D.C.—has a curious history of mixed parentage. In 1829 James Smithson, an Englishman, a graduate of Oxford and a member of the Royal Society, died in Genoa. He had never seen the United States, yet he left his estate of approximately $550,000 to our government to be used to "found at Washington under the name of the Smithsonian Institution an establishment for the increase of education and knowledge among men." It required nearly twenty years for Congress to debate the acceptance of this gift to its complete satisfaction. One wonders what additional time Congress might have required to initiate an appropriation for such a museum. Finally, in 1847, it passed a formal act establishing the institution and vested its supervision in a Board of Regents—to be composed of the Vice-President of the United States, the Chief Justice of the Supreme Court, three senators, three representatives, and six other citizens. The Smithsonian Institution now receives generous annual appropriations from Congress for the conduct of its work, but this unique museum rests solidly upon an act of the purest philanthropy—and that by a stranger.

It is interesting to recall what Mr. Smithson had in mind when he bequeathed £104,690 to found this institution in a nation he had never seen. In his will he wrote:

The best blood of England flows in my veins; on my father's side I am a Northumberland, on my mother's I am related to kings, but this avails me not. My name shall live in the memory of man when the titles of the Northumberlands and the Percys are extinct and forgotten.

Over a century later we are inclined to believe that he has achieved his desired immortality.

A remarkable story in connection with the founding of another great museum—the National Gallery of Art, in Washington—is told by Herbert Hoover in the second volume of his memoirs, *The Cabinet and The Presidency*. He relates how, while Andrew W. Mellon was in the Hoover Cabinet, the question of a certain site for a public building came up. After the Cabinet meeting Mr. Mellon came to the President and asked that the site under consideration be kept vacant. Mr. Hoover continues:

He disclosed to me his purpose to build a great national art gallery in Washington, to present to it his own collection which was to include the large number of old masters which he was then purchasing from the Soviet Government. He said he would amply endow it and thought it might altogether amount to seventy-five million dollars. I urged that he announce it at once and have the pleasure of seeing it built in his lifetime. He was a shy and modest man. The only reason he told me at all was that he wanted that site reserved. He asked me to keep it in confidence.

The National Gallery has already received other distinguished and princely gifts, such as the collection of paintings and sculptures, particularly of the Italian school, presented by the S. H. Kress Foundation. Other Kress collections are now being distributed to a score of galleries throughout the nation in order that the finest in art may be brought to the people where they live.

The Education of Women

One of the trophies of which philanthropy can be most proud is the creation of opportunities for the fullest education of women, and its part in the long train of succeeding events which liberated the sex from civil bondage. The education of women perfectly illustrates the progressive minority function which voluntary philanthropy has so often assumed. There was not the slightest hope of effective political action in their behalf until institutions independent of tax support or public vote had pioneered the way.

Girls were grossly discriminated against in our whole educational plan during the first two hundred years of colonial and national life. When the first public school was set up in Dorchester, the question arose as to whether "Maydes shall be taught with the boyes or not." For a hundred and fifty years the answer was "No." Parents were obliged to hire private tutors for their daughters or send them in groups to "Dame Schools." About 1750 a few academies—maintained by Church or private support—began to admit girls. Thus was the beginning of our coeducation, now so customary.

In the 1830's a few women began to be admitted to certain of our voluntary colleges, such as Oberlin in Ohio, Wesleyan Female College in Georgia, Mount Holyoke in Massachusetts, Rockford in Illinois, and Elmira in New York. It was at Oberlin, in September, 1837, that four young women were accepted for entrance into the Collegiate Department, with "all the instructive privileges" offered them on full academic equality with men. This event marks the beginning of coeducation on the college level.

After private philanthropy had opened college doors to women, tax-supported institutions followed the example—cautiously and hesitantly at first—at the University of Iowa in 1856 and the University of Wisconsin in 1860. Now practically every tax-supported educational institution is open to men and women alike, though some graduate schools—like medicine—long presented difficulties. Here again, we see voluntary philanthropy boldly leading the way.

SUMMER SCHOOLS

Summer schools are today a commonplace. Over three hundred regularly organized summer sessions of universities and colleges are held in the United States each year, attended largely by teachers and others who cannot leave their regular work for advanced study during the academic year. The summer school, as an important technique of adult education also, has been adopted in all English-speaking nations. Hundreds of thousands of men and women now may take regularly accredited university courses in the summer sessions.

But, again, it is to philanthropy that the world owes the earliest development of this idea: it was first launched in the summer of 1874 on the banks of Lake Chautauqua in New York, at Chautauqua Institution. Here two men—Louis Miller of Akron, father of the late Mrs. Thomas A. Edison; and Dr. John H. Vincent of Plainfield, New Jersey, later a bishop—led on by the vision of a fuller service which they could render humanity, put their own money and hard work into the establishment of an institution that loosed new impulses to personal progress and achievement. There is added interest in the fact that a young Yale teacher was the first director of the Chautauqua summer schools—Professor William R. Harper, who was soon to become the first president of the University of Chicago.

PENSIONS FOR THE AGED

Fifty years ago a proposal to pay a pension to old people, simply because they were old, would have been laughed to scorn by the great majority of voters in any state. It was a humanitarian idea just a little beyond realization through mass action. Meanwhile, influences were at work, under the stimulus of private philanthropy, which were leading slowly but surely toward acceptance of the old-age pension as a responsibility of society.

The first organized efforts in this field were made in 1717 by the Presbyterian Church. This pension system—organized by the Synod of Philadelphia—was called the Fund for Pious Uses. Presbyterians clung steadfastly to this concept of providing pensions for the aged ministers who had given their productive years, at most modest salaries, to the service of the Church. In 1927, two hundred and ten years later, they raised a philanthropic fund of fifteen million dollars, under the chairmanship of the Honorable Will H. Hays, a Presbyterian elder, with which to transform their efforts into a contributory pension system on a sound actuarial basis.

Meanwhile, other church bodies had assumed similar responsibility toward their clergy. Under the leadership of Bishop William Lawrence and J. Pierpont Morgan, the Episcopal Church had set up a contributory pension system. Through the generosity of John D. Rockefeller, the Baptist Church put into effect a similar plan.

In 1906, in the field of education, Andrew Carnegie began making a series of gifts, finally totaling over $25,000,000, to be used in creating the Carnegie Foundation for the Advancement of Teaching—one of whose primary purposes was to initiate a system of old-age pensions for college teachers of long service.

Labor took up the agitation. Great corporations recognized

their obligation to provide for men who had given a lifetime of faithful service, thus adding substantially to the well-being of American life. Today, the United States has a comprehensive plan for old-age pensions, unemployment compensation, and social security established by the Federal Government and participated in by the states and local governments. Here is a striking illustration of universal, compulsory tax support for a humanitarian idea pioneered by philanthropy from 1717 to 1935—before the people were ready to adopt it into the family of tax-supported services.

During the 1952 National Democratic Convention the following item appeared in the news dispatches:

> Among the huge placards which the Democrats have flung out here to tell the story of New Deal-Fair Deal progress is one that bears the word "charity." But "charity" is boldly crossed out and "social security" takes its place.

Obviously, the author of this demagogic reflection upon "charity" either did not know, or did not care, that for two hundred years "charity" (voluntary philanthropy) *had pioneered* in this field with its brains, its unselfish devotion, and its money before his political party could boast of the achievement of social security for the people.

SOUTHERN MOUNTAIN SCHOOLS

Within the vast area of what is termed the Southern Mountains live many of America's finest Anglo-Saxon citizens. These sturdy folk are largely descendants of the Scotch-Irish immigrants who came to the new America in the second or third wave of westward migration and who found the eastern coast so "crowded" that they went farther on into the mainland to make their new homes. Many of their descendants have been there ever since, preserving and cherishing the original concepts of American liberty and rugged individualism. President Woodrow Wilson, in a reference to the purity of the racial strain which has persisted in their geographical isolation, once suggested that perhaps a wise Providence preserved these mountain folk for a special service to the Republic in the era of social unrest and conflicting cultures which the nation has experienced in recent generations. It was voluntary philanthropy that sought out these simon-pure, strangely isolated Americans. For the past fifty years the nation has become increasingly conscious of their existence through the notable successes of voluntary institutions in carrying better educational opportunities into this region.

As a consequence, excellent schools have been established in localities which were too poor to create adequate schools by themselves. Philanthropy has pioneered a path of education through the Southern Mountains as truly as Daniel Boone once blazed the primitive trails through these same forests.

Today, systems of public education are steadily developing—still aided by foundation grants. Meanwhile, as the tax-supported development of education proceeds, voluntary sources continue to serve where especially needed. In the Southern Mountains there are still 159 schools, academies, and colleges, enrolling over 32,000 students, that are owned and supported by philanthropic agencies. Among these students there may be—who knows?—future Abraham Lincolns, David Farraguts, Alvin Yorks, who will render vital service to the Republic they love so intensely.

CITY FIRE DEPARTMENTS

Our present-day city fire department, with its highly trained, smartly uniformed force and its magnificent mechanized fire-fighting equipment, is a modern outgrowth of volunteer community effort. The older generation, particularly those of us who grew up in smaller communities, well remember the volunteer fire departments formed by local citizens banding together for the mutual protection of their homes. Some have at least heard of, or seen in the movies, the old "bucket line" that passed pails of water along by hand.

Taxation is a fairly recent device for supporting a community fire department. For generations in America, while the only organized fire-fighting companies were volunteers, all funds for their equipment and operation were raised by personal contributions or by picnics, ice-cream "socials," auctions, bazaars, carnivals, and other community fund-raising devices.

In July of 1952 *The New York Times* thus reported on the

200th-anniversary celebration of what is said to be the oldest volunteer fire company in the nation—Relief Fire Company No. 1, of Mt. Holly, New Jersey:

Six thousand firemen and auxiliary members representing 158 New Jersey, Pennsylvania, Delaware and Maryland fire companies marched today in a four-hour parade as the climax of the 200th anniversary program of the nation's oldest volunteer fire company that can boast of continuous service.

The paraders, paced by forty bands, marched through the streets of this community, which this week honored Relief Fire Company No. 1. The company was organized here on July 11, 1752, when Mount Holly was known as Bridgetown. The week-long program ended tonight with a fireworks display. Prizes were given to competing companies in the line of march.

Here we see another of America's notable nongovernmental civic endeavors. The unselfish and hazardous service given through the years by thousands of volunteer fire companies is one of the most striking demonstrations of spontaneous, self-disciplined American co-operation for the good of all in a community.

This account of some of the civic, educational, humanitarian, and cultural developments for which we are indebted to generous American philanthropy has already grown longer than was anticipated. Other significant projects could be cited—ranging the wide arc of human endeavor, from the fight against hookworm to the movement for better homes—but space does not permit. We must end this recital, not for lack of material but because of its abundance.

The account leads one to the realization that philanthropy has played a striking role in the development of our American society. As a corollary, it seems to me that it deserves—upon the record of its past achievements—the sympathy, the co-operation, and the generosity of all well-disposed citizens. These are the citizens who love our Republic, who are proud of its present high place in the society of nations, and who want to have a share in its increasing service to mankind.

PART THREE

Why Do Men Give?

CHAPTER VII

The Church—The Greatest Philanthropic Force in American Life

FOR those who may question this chapter title, let us recall some facts of American history.

First, it was a powerful religious motive that led to the founding of the Colonies and set the decisive pattern of our civilization. In sharp contrast, attempts at conquest for the sake of gold almost faded out as influences in the life of what was to become the United States.

The new nation was organized by men of faith. As every schoolchild is taught, even our minted coins testify that "In God We Trust." Every proclamation, every official assembly, bears the same witness.

The Christian faith was considered so essential a factor in our civilization that unbelievably difficult and heroic efforts were made, by both Catholic and Protestant missionaries, to implant it also among the Indians.

Later, our Declaration of Independence, as we are often reminded, traced our inalienable rights—"Life, Liberty and the pursuit of Happiness"—to one source, the Creator.

That we remain a "religious nation" has even been confirmed by our highest legal authority—the United States Supreme Court. This opinion does not decree that we *must* be; it recognizes that we *are*. Strong popular confirmation of this attitude could hardly be missed in President Eisenhower's inauguration. Not only did the throng facing the Capitol sincerely join him in "a little private prayer" of his own, but the spiritual response swept across the country. The following day newspapers everywhere recorded the fact. The *New York Herald Tribune*, in a story headed "All Faiths Here Offer Prayers for Eisenhower," had this significant paragraph:

Protestants, Catholics and Jews, in their prayers and special services, *called attention to the fact that since the United States is entrusted to God's care,* its citizens must live up to this high purpose if they wish to receive the gifts of peace and prosperity.

If then, as commonly admitted, this is essentially a Christian nation; if the twin pillars of faith and action are the Fatherhood of God and the Brotherhood of Man; and if the churches of America have remained close to the practical lives of their people, as they have done—what more natural than that the Church, in all its wide sweep, should be "the greatest philanthropic force in American life."

The Judaeo-Christian religion, throughout its centuries of development, has been the world's greatest teacher of justice and mercy; of the laws of God, and of His love for all men. Philanthropy—the love of mankind—is its natural fruitage.

If we ask, then, why do men give, the best answer is that much of the motivation, probably 90 per cent of it, comes from religion—as taught and inspired by our organized churches and as put into action, however imperfectly, by their members and adherents.

This is not to claim that every generous giver is, *ipso facto,* an active church man. Indeed, there are many generous men and women of our generation who do not lay claim to any positive religious conviction. However, even in these cases the chances are about 99 to 1, I believe, that their parents and grandparents were religious men and women and that they are still living on the spiritual resources of their forbears. Or, as one young lady remarked, "They are riding on their Mother's ticket."

The Christian Church has proved to be the most creative agency in American life. It deserves far better understanding of the immense service it has rendered our developing civilization. There was a time—only a short generation ago—when the public needed no such reminder. When I was a boy, the church was easily the central institution in our community. Social, cultural, recreational, and community life revolved about it. My father, a Congregationalist minister, was the most highly respected man in our town; men touched their hats when they met him—not in tribute to him personally, for he was a most modest man, but to the high office which he held as a minister of the Church of Christ.

SOME BY-PRODUCTS

To suggest the creative influence of religious conviction, I propose to recall some of the notable by-products of the Church in American life. They go back many years.

The progress which we have made in the past century toward *world peace*, for instance, is a definite by-product of the Church. In 1815 a small group of Christian laymen and ministers organized the first peace organization in the world—the American Peace Society. It is still in existence, by the way. Within a few years, the British Peace Society was organized, *La Société des Amis de Morale Chrétienne* was founded in Paris, and the Geneva Peace Society was founded in Switzerland—all by Church members in these nations. These four societies led the Western World in the formation of sentiment against war, initiating a series of international conferences in London, Paris, Geneva, and elsewhere which have become a vital technique in international relations today.

As a matter of fact, nearly all present-day activity against war can be definitely traced back to the work of these organized groups. They took as their text the words of the Hebrew prophet: "They shall beat their swords into plowshares." As a result of their hundred-year agitation, we now have the Pan-American Union, the World Court, the United Nations, a partial system of arbitration, a start toward the codification of international law, and a growing demand for co-operation as a substitute for war.

Another supremely important by-product of the Church in America is the *abolition of human slavery*. The first antislavery society in the world of which I find mention was organized in 1775 in Philadelphia by Quakers. It was called the Pennsylvania Society for Promoting the Abolition of Slavery, the Relief of Free Negroes Unlawfully Held in Bondage, and for Improving the Condition of the African Race. (This amply titled society still exists.) Twelve years later, English Quakers founded a sister

British society. As a result of the determined opposition of the latter, slavery was abolished in Great Britain in 1835.

In this country Church people of all denominations took up the fight; within a generation there were 140 antislavery societies, 106 of them in the South. George Trevelyan, the historian, has called the work of these Church antislavery societies "a turning point in the history of the world"; for, said he, "if slavery had continued into the industrial half of the 19th Century, the tropics would have become a vast slave farm for human exploitation and the European races would have been degraded by the diseases of slave-civilization of which the Roman Empire died."

So many direct and indirect by-products of the Christian Church come to mind that it is hard to choose those most deserving of mention. Since several of them have already been described in Chapter VI—itself an expression of faith in the Fatherhood of God and the brotherhood of man—they need only brief mention here.

There are our *hospitals*, which have already been discussed. Even the old religions of Egypt, Greece, and India produced hospitals. Crude though they were, they were the only institutions of mercy for the sick, while for many centuries in the Christian era the only hospitals in the Western World were those provided by the Church.

Welfare work—the concern for the poor and disadvantaged— is a by-product of the Church's patient pioneering during the past hundred years. First, Church people organized rescue and aid societies; then, in the 1840's, they created the Association for Improving the Condition of the Poor—the well-known A.I.C.P. —in many cities. Later, Protestant groups established their modern welfare societies which taught the nation a new sense of social responsibility and better methods. The Catholic Church has been equally active in the social service field with its diocesan charities, and its St. Vincent de Paul and numerous other societies. The Jewish people have carried on a marvelous program of welfare work both through their own numerous societies and through their active support of civic projects.

Then there is the enormous range of youth movements and *character-building agencies* created and maintained by Church people. Our Young Men's and Young Women's Christian Associations, Catholic Youth groups, Hebrew associations, Boy Scouts, Girl Scouts, boys' clubs, settlement houses, and many others have a membership of about five million boys and girls, young men and women, whose characters and personalities are being thoughtfully trained by devoted leaders.

Practically all *formal education* in America was initiated by the Christian Church, as already described. Most of our secondary schools and many of our primary schools were denominational institutions during the first two hundred years of American life. Even in the great city of New York—a secular spot if there is one—public education was a "charity" carried on by religious and philanthropic organizations until the present City Board of Education was organized about a hundred years ago.

As for *higher education* in America, we have seen that it was peculiarly a by-product of religious forces—all but one of the ten colleges founded prior to the Revolution being organized by ministers and under religious auspices. The missionary zeal and the sacrifice which went into the founding of these Church-related colleges are almost beyond belief. In the records of Bucknell University we actually read of a subscription of twenty-five cents, payable in four annual installments, made by an earnest Baptist.

Learning to Give

The Church is the chief agency which systematically tries to teach people to give, starting this unique process even with its youngest children. It teaches Cradle Roll children in the Sunday Schools of Protestant churches, and similarly the tiniest tots in Catholic churches and Jewish synagogues, to bring their pennies for special missionary offerings. Through all the teaching and preaching of the clergy runs the theme of stewardship: man has what he possesses as but a steward of God and should use it to serve God and humanity. It is the Church which almost alone carries the burden of persuading people to give unselfishly and systematically to altruistic activities. Religion is truly the mother of philanthropy—a mother of great faith and great patience, glad when her children carry on her work.

For example: a generation ago a Chinese boy attended two Presbyterian schools which had been established by American missionaries in northern China. This boy prospered in manhood and a few years ago gave a million dollars to the Presbyterian Church in America—"in gratitude to God for my Christian education in life, and in appreciation of the services missionaries have given to China."

He stipulated that the funds should be used to build a home in Southern California for retired Presbyterian foreign missionaries. That home has been created. Called Westminster Gardens, it is located at Duarte, at the foot of the Sierra Madre Mountains. Thirty-five Presbyterian missionaries are now spending their retirement years in this beautiful retreat, paying a nominal rental of only $35 to $55 per month, because of the generosity of this Chinese businessman.

It is impossible to name this generous Chinese who reversed the customary missionary "westward-to-eastward" flow of generosity, for the only string he attached to his gift was that his name remain undisclosed.

EARLY "ESTABLISHMENT" OF RELIGION

It is interesting to note in connection with this reference to the Church itself as the largest single enterprise in America supported by voluntary gifts that it was not always so supported here. The Pilgrims and the Puritans who came to New England in the early part of the seventeenth century left England and the Continent in part because of their resentment at being obliged to pay taxes to support the established Church from which they so strongly dissented. They did not want the Church supported or presided over by the state, and when they first came to Massachusetts they decreed that their ministers should be supported solely by voluntary contributions. In a pioneer country, this proved difficult.

In order to meet the problem of meager voluntary support, laws were passed about 1650 which levied a special tax—or "ministerial rate," as it was called—for the support of churches and clergymen. Thus, the Church in New England became a tax-supported institution, and the very people who had traveled three thousand miles across a stormy sea to escape the dictation of one established Church made the Congregational Church the established Church in their new home.

Nearly two hundred years were required to terminate completely all tax support of the Church in New England, and to make it the wholly voluntary institution it now is nationally; although in the Middle Atlantic States the Quakers, the Presbyterians, and the Dutch Reformists saw to it that the Church was from the beginning a voluntary institution.

The mortal blow was given the whole policy of tax-supported churches in 1789 when the Constitution for the new Republic was adopted—the first Amendment to which provided that "Congress shall make no law respecting the establishment of religion or prohibiting the free exercise thereof." The objection was not to the recognition of religion, but to its support by compulsory taxation. Finally, in 1830, religion in New England was placed upon the same voluntary basis upon which it rested in the rest of the United States, and from that time to this all churches in America have been supported chiefly by the gifts of those who give because they love the Church and wish to aid it in its service to God and man.

VOLUNTARY GIVING INCREASES

Some might perhaps have expected that the sequel to that action would read something like this: "And so, after the compulsion of giving to churches was removed, they declined in support and activity, for people do not give voluntarily to the cause of religion." But, as everyone knows, the exact opposite was the result: in subsequent years all three major divisions of organized religion in the United States have gained immensely in numbers, in the value of their holdings, and in the breadth of their activity. The more completely voluntary giving to churches became, the greater became the generosity of the people. As a consequence, there is no institution in America today on a sounder financial basis than the Church. F. Emerson Andrews estimates in his book, *Philanthropic Giving* (published by the Russell Sage Foundation), that the value of the property and endowment owned by the religious organizations of America totals approximately ten billion dollars.

By and large, the churches have conducted their financial affairs with great care and the utmost probity. For the most part they have not built their new edifices on borrowed money. At the time of the last religious census, the debt of all the churches in the United States was only 11.3 per cent of the total value of the edifices. What other business has been so conservative? As a result of this careful management of their fiscal affairs the churches in America weathered the 1929 depression with great credit. While one of every six banks slipped into bankruptcy and one of twenty-two businesses went out of existence, and $1 of each $18 worth of municipal bonds went by default, only 1 in 2,344 churches lost its property through foreclosure. During the same period the membership of most of the nation's social organizations was deflated alarmingly—many of them losing from 20 per cent to 60 per cent of their active members—yet the churches added substantially to their membership.

These wholly voluntary American institutions, although entirely dependent upon the gifts of men and women free to withdraw their support at any moment, are so entrenched in the lives and hearts of their members that their support goes steadily on, even when people feel themselves obliged to curtail many other expenditures of a personal or selfish nature. People give to their churches and, through them, to countless other benevolent agencies because they want to.

Especially in the case of independent colleges this same deep loyalty comes to light, as those familiar with these institutions have good cause to know. An interesting example is that of Atwood Manley, the publisher (now retired) of the St. Lawrence *Plaindealer* of Canton, New York.

Recently St. Lawrence University, his Alma Mater, called a meeting of a score of the college's friends in an endeavor to have them take the lead in raising a much-needed development fund. President Eugene Bewkes described the needs.

In the course of the discussion Mr. Manley said, "I'd like to tell you a story. About fifty years ago I—then a small boy—saw President Gunnison and a group of the faculty and other friends of the college doing something on the campus and, boylike, I investigated. President Gunnison had a spade; after a short ceremony he proceeded to turn over several spadefuls of earth. I pressed in closer to see better and the President, noticing me, motioned for me to come and take the spade and go on with what he was doing. I did, and then he said, 'Atwood, you are young and will, I hope, live many years after most of us are gone. You will always remember this day, and I want you fifty years from now to do some more spade work for this beloved College!' "

Mr. Manley concluded, "Now I am ready to do what spade work the college wants of me in this development program." And so, it proved, was everyone else present—stimulated and inspired by words a devoted president had spoken a half century previously. Thus are men moved to give.

WHY DO MEN NOT GIVE?

Before closing this discussion of why men give, I shall try to throw some light on the subject by recalling instances of men who did *not give.* I have already related one instance in Chapter II of a man who held before him all his life a selfish ideal of constantly increasing his fortune—for its own sake—and thus failed to experience the joy and satisfaction of giving.

There was another successful businessman in a Midwestern city, an alumnus and trustee of a college which was trying to raise a substantial capital fund. When the president of his Alma Mater asked him for his contribution, the trustee excused himself for a few minutes, during which he inspected carefully his portfolio of investments. Returning to the interviewer, he announced that he could not give anything because he found all of his investments in prime condition and had no "bad" stocks to discard! He was a bit like the housewife who, when asked to make a donation to the church supper, picked out a can of fruit slightly spoiled which she thought she could spare.

Dr. Claude M. Fuess, headmaster emeritus of Phillips Academy, Andover, Massachusetts, tells in his autobiography about a man whom he solicited for a gift to the Academy. Dr. Fuess stressed the need for funds by emphasizing that the Academy had had an operating deficit the year before. "A deficit?" asked the man. "A deficit? I guess you need a new management."

There was also a man whom I never saw, and that is part of this anecdote. He was a trustee of a little college in a southern town which was about to launch a campaign for a modest, but badly needed, capital fund. He was the wealthy man of the town; his mother, his wife, and his daughters were all alumnae of the college and the family was devoted to the institution. He was an active trustee and, as such, had voted for the college to launch the campaign. But as the time for the solicitation drew nearer, he became more and more nervous. I was due to arrive in the town on a certain day to attend the opening dinner of the campaign, but when the occasion came to pass Mr. Trustee was not present. He was home in bed—sick and worn out from the thought of the money he would be asked to give. I learned later that he made a good recovery after the campaign closed. I have often wondered if he got as much from the use of the money he saved as he would have enjoyed had he given it to the college.

CHAPTER VIII

The American "Westminster Abbey"

TO MANY Americans, the most impressive spot in England is Westminster Abbey. There, one is gazing upon ageless memorials to men and women whose stories have been woven into our common heritage. The names of poets, warriors, artists, kings, and empire builders are enshrined there. Paris and Rome have their Pantheon, Spain its Escorial, and Germany its Valhalla—all similarly filled with inscriptions and memorials to those who have been thought worthy of remembrance.

We of the United States have no comparable national memorial. Rather, we are preserving the names and records of a host of the finest men and women of each generation through living memorials established in connection with our philanthropic institutions. Our colleges, our churches, our hospitals, our orphan asylums, our settlements, our libraries, our museums, our cathedrals—the whole network of cultural, humanitarian, and religious edifices maintained by the voluntary gifts of our people—comprise a vast "Westminster Abbey" of living memorials. Contained under no single roof, it reaches out—under thousands of roofs—to every section of our land.

One can scarcely appreciate the extent of this vast "Westminster Abbey" until one tries to estimate the number and variety of these individual memorials—from the inscriptions "To the Loving Memory of my Father and Mother" on the stained-glass window of the village church to the great Gothic Harkness Tower at Yale, erected to the memory of a brother.

The endowments undergirding the structures of our philanthropic institutions also contain a myriad of specific memorial units. A hospital or college catalogue may contain pages of such endowment units, ranging from $50 to $10,000,000 in size, each given in memory of a relative or friend whom the donor wished to honor. There are at least a million people of past generations whose names are thus treasured. Their humanitarian service is being carried on for generations after their own earthly lives are ended, through visible and invisible memorials built into the daily activity of philanthropic institutions.

The memorial feature of a philanthropic gift is often an important factor in the purpose of the giver. Seldom does a person make a gift for the purpose of selfishly memorializing himself, but often he is moved to make a larger gift when he realizes that he can serve a needy cause and, at the same time, honor the name of family or friends. Any permanent philanthropic institution which wishes to attract substantial gifts does well to offer such opportunities for dignified memorials. One never fully knows the specific motives that inspire given individuals to make notable gifts, but it is certain that the memorial feature is, in many cases, a strong—if not a decisive—factor.

EXAMPLES ARE MANY AND DIVERSE

Recently, the officers of the Lutheran Church Home for the Aged in Buffalo, New York, asked the members of the Evangelical Lutheran churches in western New York to make gifts of $175,000 to build an additional wing to the half-century-old "Haven of Refuge at Eventide." A list of thirty-nine rooms was offered as memorial gift possibilities, ranging in cost from $1,000 to $17,500. All of these rooms were adopted as memorials by donors, and over each room has been placed a bronze plate inscribed in honor of a loved one whom the donor wished to have remembered across the years in connection with this unselfish service to those for whom the Psalmist of old pleaded in these moving words:

> Cast me not off in the time of old age;
> Forsake me not when my strength faileth.

Not only can colleges, hospitals, and other institutions point to various memorial buildings, halls, or rooms, but many such establishments are themselves—in their entirety—memorials to founders or donors who have made notable gifts at a critical period. One hundred and sixty-five colleges in America are so named. There are also 450 hospitals named after the persons whose generosity helped to found them. There are 4,000 libraries named for donors—nearly 3,000 of them, if you please, named for one man, Andrew Carnegie.

On the seal of one of the great universities of America, if not of the world—the University of Chicago—are the words "Founded by John D. Rockefeller." That memorial will be full of meaning, I dare say, to generations to which the name Standard Oil Company may be but a myth, for succeeding generations have a curious habit of remembering how men *use* their money long after they have forgotten how they *made* it.

Few of us could now say how the richest man in the America of the Revolutionary period—George Washington—acquired his wealth; but all of us know that he used his wealth and his influence in the service of his country. Among other things, he used it in the service of philanthropy—especially of the dozen colleges that today bear his name, including Washington College at Chestertown, Maryland, in which he took an especial interest. One was renamed for him because it was saved by his gift. That was the little school, originally called Liberty Hall Academy, at Lexington, Virginia. When George Washington gave the struggling school $10,000 its name was changed to Washington Academy, and later to Washington College. Still later on, it became Washington and Lee University, in honor of General Robert E. Lee, who, after his surrender to General Grant, gladly accepted the presidency of the proud little college that was about to close its doors because of poverty. Washington and Lee University now splendidly serves as a joint memorial to Virginia's two great sons.

Among other colleges which are memorials to generous donors are the following well-known institutions: Harvard, the story of whose naming after John Harvard has already been told; Yale, named after Elihu Yale; William and Mary, named for King William and Queen Mary; Brown, which was called Rhode Island College until 1805, when its name was changed in honor of a donor of $5,000; Smith, a common enough name, but that of a most uncommon little lady of Massachusetts who gave $300,-000 for the founding of a woman's college; Duke, named for Washington Duke, as earlier recounted here; Bucknell, once the

University of Lewisburg until the generosity of William Bucknell of Philadelphia led the trustees to change its name; Tulane, named in honor of Paul Tulane; Johns Hopkins, a great memorial to a Baltimore gentleman of that name—both of these latter gifts probably inspired by the public benevolences of George Peabody; Washburn, of Kansas, originally Lincoln College, but changed to memorialize a generous Massachusetts family; Dartmouth, once called Moor's Indian Charity School until a financial agent of the college went to England and received a gift of $10,000 from Lord Dartmouth.

Some of the great hospitals of the land also stand out as memorials to individual donors: Payne Whitney Clinic at the Cornell University Medical Center in New York, a memorial to Mr. Whitney, who gave millions to the institution; Bob Roberts Memorial Hospital for Children in Chicago, given by Mr. and Mrs. John Roberts as a memorial to their five-year-old son; the Collis P. Huntington Memorial Hospital of Boston, given by Mrs. Huntington as a memorial to her husband; the Baker Memorial Hospital of Boston, made possible by the bequest of a million dollars from the estate of Mrs. Mary Richardson in memory of her parents, Mr. and Mrs. Richard Baker, Jr.

Also, the Lankenau Hospital of Philadelphia, a memorial to John D. Lankenau, a generous and useful Philadelphia citizen of seventy-five years ago; Barnes Hospital of St. Louis, in honor of Robert A. Barnes, who left his estate for this purpose; the Charles T. Miller Hospital of St. Paul, named for the man who left a million and a half to the institution; the Henrietta Eccleston Hospital for Children in Atlanta, the gift of Thomas Eccleston in loving memory of his mother; the Scripps Memorial Hospital at La Jolla, California, the gift of Ellen Browning Scripps; the John D. Archbold Hospital of Thomasville, Georgia —and so on, to a length which space does not permit.

Let me recall only a few other types of philanthropic institutions established as individual or family memorials. The Hershey Industrial Institution at Hershey, Pennsylvania, has received property and money to the value of sixty million dollars from the late Mr. and Mrs. Milton Hershey, of chocolate fame. The Astor, Lenox, and Tilden libraries—now combined in the great New

York Public Library at Fifth Avenue and Forty-second Street—
were the individual gifts or bequests of John Jacob Astor, James
Lenox, and Samuel J. Tilden. The Pratt Institute of Brooklyn
is the gift of the Pratt family, one of the founders of the Standard
Oil Company. This great corporation produced not only wealth
for its founders, but inspired philanthropic gifts in so many of
the families connected with it in the early days that their roster
contains the names of many of America's most general philanthropists—Rockefeller, Harkness, Severance, Pratt, Archbold,
Bostwick, and many others.

How Effective Is a Memorial?

If one is in any doubt as to whether a memorial gift actually
preserves the memory of individuals whose names might otherwise have been long forgotten, the following test is suggested:

Do you know this man? Born in Massachusetts in 1795, he went
to the District of Columbia at the age of fifteen and entered
the wholesale mercantile business. At nineteen, he opened up
his own dry-goods establishment at Georgetown, and started one
of the first express companies in America, carrying parcels between Washington, Baltimore, and Philadelphia. He became
successful and prosperous, and in 1837 the ramifications of his
business took him to London, where he made his home thereafter.

He became immensely wealthy; gave a museum to Harvard
and another to Yale. It was he who started the Charity Organization Society in London, with a gift of $2,500,000. He was a
friend of Queen Victoria in England and of President Lincoln in
America, and when he died in 1868 he was probably the most
widely known civilian in the world. The Queen sent his body
home to America aboard a British warship, which was met here
by an escort headed by Admiral Farragut. Congress struck a
special medal in his honor.

Surely, such a man should be remembered only eighty-five
years after his death. But, as a matter of fact, not one in a million
could name him, so fleeting is our recollection of people who are
gone. But there are institutions in America which will see to it
that his memory is always kept alive. These bear his name: five

libraries, a museum in Baltimore, endowment funds in seven universities of America, a great educational institution—*George Peabody* College, at Nashville, Tennessee—the great teacher-training institution of the South.

Or take this test. A five-year-old boy came with his parents from England to New York State in 1796. His father was a brewer, but the brewery burned in 1811; in 1812 the young man, then only twenty-one, started a brewery of his own. He became wealthy and gave generous sums to the various enterprises of the Baptist denomination of which he was an earnest member. Like George Peabody, he died in 1868, highly respected and honored by his generation.

You never heard of him? Oh, yes, you have. His name was *Matthew Vassar.* You know the name well because he gave a half million dollars to found America's first fully organized woman's college.

Will you take another test? In 1807 a boy was born of Quaker parents in Westchester County, New York. He enjoyed little or no formal education and went to work early as a carpenter and a machinist. He became interested in telegraphy in the early days of that invention, and later became one of the founders of the Western Union Telegraph Company. He lost a fortune at one time in an endeavor to lay telegraph wires underground from Washington to New York.

Achieving a distinguished career in business and in public life, he was recognized at his death in 1878 as one of the outstanding men of the Empire State. You never heard of him? Oh, yes, you have, for his name—*Ezra Cornell*—is immortalized by the great institution on Cayuga Lake, to the founding of which he gave sums totaling over two million dollars.

And what of the lad born on Staten Island—son of a truck farmer—who at the age of sixteen bought a sailboat and began to carry produce across from Staten Island to New York City? This boyish beginning grew into a ferry system and a little railroad line which finally became America's richest and most extensive railroad system. You are familiar, of course, with the name, for various descendants of his are active in the social and business life of our generation. But at Nashville, Tennessee, a

great institution of learning—Vanderbilt University—will probably preserve the name and memory of *Cornelius Vanderbilt,* its
donor-founder, longer than will any business enterprise associated
with the family name.

Still another test! There was a lad born in upstate New York
in 1824 who worked hard throughout his youth, developed conspicuous business ability, and was one of the men who shortly
after the Civil War took part in building the Union Pacific Railroad through and around the Rockies to the Pacific Coast. He
entered political life and became a distinguished United States
senator from California. There are thousands still living who
knew him intimately, and yet few except his close friends could
identify him from this brief description. But there is scarcely
an educated person in America who is not familiar with his
name, for he gave twenty million dollars to found a university
in loving memory of a young son who had died. You know him
now—for the University was named for the boy, *Leland Stan-
ford,* Jr.

This custom of embodying philanthropic gifts in permanent
memorials to the givers is no American discovery. It has been
practiced for centuries. Many of the colleges at Oxford and
Cambridge are such memorials. One of the most striking and
dramatic examples is that of a college at Cambridge founded
in 1347 by Mary de Saint Paul—celebrated in English history
as "maid, wife, and widow in a single day." As story has it, her
wedding day was celebrated by one of the thrilling knightly
tournaments of that period and her knight—the Earl of Pembroke, to whom she had been married but a few hours—fell
before the lance of his opponent. In loving, grief-stricken memory
of the Earl, the young bride-widow gave funds to establish *Pembroke* College.

For six hundred years Pembroke has been rendering living
service to the cause of civilization, in the name of the young
Earl and in honor of the generous woman who sought to assuage
her grief by a humanitarian act. Among the men whom this
memorial gift educated to the benefit of the race were Edmund
Spenser, England's gentle poet; Archbishop Nicholas Ridley, a
martyr, with Cranmer, to the Protestant religion; William Pitt,

the great liberal statesman; and, in our own nation, Roger Williams, valiant young knight who never hesitated to tilt his own lance in the cause of religious liberty.

When the world's richest man, John D. Rockefeller, Sr., decided to devote his wealth to the service of God and humanity, he engaged a learned man to study the experience of giving in the past and to make recommendations, based on such studies, for the placement of his money to serve humanity best. Incorporated in this scholarly report was the following significant passage:

Money given for endowment tends to perpetuate the usefulness of the donor through all time. His gift confers upon him an immortality of usefulness. Through it, he becomes a permanent prop of civilization, an ever-living force in human progress. Endowments then offer mighty motives to the giver. Here, if nowhere else, he sees himself achieving immortality. Endowments appeal with resistless force to that love of life, eternal life, which is the prime instinct of our being.

These words sum up ages of human experience and wisdom. They explain, in convincing language, the deep appeal in giving to our philanthropic institutions in America. Such gifts are rendered doubly inspiring because they link the vision of perpetual unselfish service with the feeling that such service is the most worthy possible tribute to one whose memory the giver wishes to honor. In our far-flung American "Westminster Abbey" —filled with its significant memorials—philanthropy preserves a sort of national roster of that great company of high-minded men and women of every generation who are akin through their desire to serve and bless mankind.

How Are Philanthropic Funds Raised?

PART FOUR

How Are Philanthropic Funds Raised?

CHAPTER IX

The Old-Time Financial Agent and the Modern Development Program

UP TO this point we have been considering philanthropy *itself*. We have tried first to define and describe it, to search out its inner springs, to see how it works. We found that the evidence points clearly to religion—solid convictions about the Fatherhood of God and the brotherhood of man—as the main source of motive power. Evidently the love of God has consistently generated love of our fellow men and a practical concern for their good.

We then surveyed typical fruits of philanthropy, especially those produced in our own country. We found their number so large as to justify the conclusion that voluntary philanthropy has been the pioneer in the main fields of civilization's progress.

To give philanthropy's role the concreteness and personal color that it has in actual life, we also recounted the stories of a number of our citizens whose vision, warm humanity, and means have contributed so much to the America of which we are justly proud.

We now face three major questions of interest to all who are concerned with philanthropy's share in American civilization:

How have gifts been secured in the past?

What are the current trends in giving?

How may the tested methods of the past be applied, and new approaches developed, so as to stimulate an increased flow of voluntary giving to match the growing opportunities and needs?

Let us now seek answers to these and the many related questions.

As some men are sufficiently moved by an inner compulsion to give freely to humanitarian causes, there are others who must be shown the ways of stewardship. There are many men—themselves unable to see visions—who believe earnestly in the dreams of others and are happy to support their causes. In many cases personal presentation is needed to make them aware of their opportunity and duty to give. Here, the financial agent enters into the program.

THE OLDEST OF METHODS

The employment of a financial agent to go about personally soliciting gifts is the oldest technique for raising philanthropic funds. Long before the printing press was invented or the postal system created—out of which two developments has grown the modern direct mail appeal—the financial agent was a recognized officer of most charitable institutions. A thousand years ago a permanent officer of such medieval charities was designated as the financial agent, or proctor. It was his duty to travel over the domain pleading for gifts and bequests. The success of this method of personal solicitation is proved by the enormous endowments and properties which many of the medieval universities, hospitals, and monasteries accumulated.

Our own early voluntary institutions invariably employed a financial agent to call personally upon men and women of means, searching diligently wherever there was prospect of finding contributors to the cause he represented. Often, also, he preached in the pulpits on Sundays, for philanthropic giving was closely related to the churches. In the early history of our Colonial colleges, the president himself was the most effective financial agent—a precedent which has obtained in many instances down to the present day.

To most persons the task of going about to solicit money was as distasteful then as it is now, and it was not always easy for the early American colleges to get the man they wanted for president, because of this unpleasant duty that devolved upon him. For this reason Yale was at one time without a president for four years. It required a courageous type of man in those days—as it does today—to be a college president.

Dr. John Witherspoon was such a man. When he assumed the presidency of Princeton he took to the road with genuine enthusiasm, becoming the great fund raiser of Princeton's early days. Up and down the land he went, preaching in the principal Presbyterian pulpits on Sunday and calling upon laymen during the week. As a result he succeeded in strengthening Princeton's financial position as greatly as he enlarged her prestige and enriched her intellectual life. Witherspoon was so aggressive a solicitor and propagandist that he even addressed a vigorous appeal for Princeton funds "to the inhabitants and others of the West India Islands."

Benjamin Franklin tells, with his own particular zest, numerous stories of his experiences in soliciting his fellow citizens of Philadelphia for various nongovernmental civic enterprises, including the forerunner of the University of Pennsylvania. When the Reverend Gilbert Tennent came to him to ask his help in raising a fund to build a Presbyterian church, Franklin was unwilling to solicit his fellow citizens for the purpose, but tried to be as helpful as possible without taking part in the actual solicitation. The advice he gave Mr. Tennent, although now nearly two hundred years old, is as fresh and useful as the day he gave it. Franklin thus wrote of the occasion:

I said, "In the first place I advise you to apply to all those whom you know will give something; next, to those whom you are uncertain whether they will give anything or not, and show them the list of those who have given; and lastly, do not neglect those whom you are sure will give nothing, for in some of them you may be mistaken."

He laughed and thanked me, and said he would take my advice. He did so, for he asked everybody, and he obtained a much larger sum than he expected, with which he erected the capacious and very elegant meeeting-house that stands in Arch Street.

WHERE DID THEY SEEK GIFTS?

An interesting thing about the financial agents who represented America's philanthropic institutions is that, for the most part, they moved eastward—even across the water to Europe. In Colonial days, of course, it was especially so. The early history of our pre-Revolutionary colleges contains numerous records of an action something like this: "And so the trustees, having exhausted their own resources, called upon Mr. Blank to make a journey to England and Scotland to ask our friends there to send us more financial aid." Harvard repeatedly sent her financial agents to solicit funds in England. In a number of its first hundred and fifty years financial agents obtained more money for Harvard in England than the college received from all its friends in this country.

The Reverend John Blair was sent to England as the financial agent for William and Mary, succeeding there in raising substantial sums, as mentioned in a previous chapter. Benjamin Franklin and his fellow founders of the University of Pennsylvania sent their agents to England and to France as well, where Franklin had made many friends. Eleazer Wheelock's financial emissary to England obtained a handsome gift from Lord Dartmouth, for whom the college was renamed.

In a dark day of Princeton's history, the trustees sent two of their members to England—Gilbert Tennent and Samuel Davies. Tennent had already shown his capacity to solicit funds, but Davies undertook the unpleasant task with heavy heart. He started the trip with "very gloomy prospects." How often have other financial agents gone about their unwelcome job in the same cheerless frame of mind! In this case, however, their forebodings were not justified, for the two men together raised £3,200 in Scotland, England, and Ireland—and the fund which they brought back was used to build Old Nassau Hall.

Dr. John Jones went to England in 1771 for the Society of the Hospital in this City of New York in America—there to solicit funds for the establishment of New York's first general hospital, the present New York Hospital at the Cornell University Medical Center. With the help of the ubiquitous and persuasive Benjamin Franklin, who chanced to be in London at the time, he succeeded in obtaining some generous gifts.

CULTIVATING NEW FIELDS

After the American Revolution, financial agents naturally ceased to find much support in England for institutions over here. President Witherspoon of Princeton had the temerity to try it once in 1783, but he found the feeling in the mother country so strong against America—and specifically against himself for his active part in the Revolution—that he did not raise enough money to pay for the trip. Edwin Norris, in his book *The Story of Princeton,* says: "At that time Dr. Witherspoon was about as popular in England as a Hessian soldier would have been at an American Fourth of July celebration."

After American civilization started to spread westward, pioneering and colonizing leaders proceeded to establish various philanthropic institutions on the advancing frontier—naturally sending their financial agents back East for needed funds to the settled and wealthy centers of population. The financial agents of this period were almost always ministers. Their technique was to preach in the churches, perhaps taking up a collection at the services; and then, during the week, to try to secure gifts from individuals of means in the community. This custom is still followed by many institutions, especially those located in the less settled portions of the nation.

Until recently a score or more financial agents of out-of-town institutions were to be found on any given day in New York and other large eastern cities endeavoring to call personally, either at office or home, on substantial men and women who had shown an interest in cultural and religious undertakings. Often much thought had previously gone into developing these particular interests.

Today the western colleges do not turn to New York and Boston as they used to because the South and the West now have their own indigenous wealth and are well able to support their own educational institutions. As a matter of fact, college presidents from the great Empire State of New York and the Commonwealth of Pennsylvania—as well as from New England—have in recent years made pilgrimages to Texas to seek funds for their eastern institutions. Their success, however, has not been such as to inspire emulation, for the new wealth of Texas seems reluctant to do philanthropic duty outside the Lone Star State. In fact, Texas imposes a penalty on gifts made to philanthropic institutions outside the state, in the following manner:

In the State of Texas there is no reciprocal statute allowing a tax exemption for gifts to eleemosynary causes outside the State.

Testamentary gifts for philanthropic purposes for use beyond the State line are taxable. As a consequence, charitable bequests of decedents, if they are to avoid the tax, must be limited to use within the State. Similarly, a foundation receiving testamentary bequests would be restricted to use within the State.

It is not an easy life. The financial agent meets a rebuff here and an insult there, discouragement and lack of sympathy on every side. But occasionally the door of an office, and the gateway of a heart, opens—and his beloved institution is given a subscription which repays him for many days of patient, if apparently unrewarding, effort.

SOME TRUE STORIES

Some amazing but true stories can be told of the successes of financial agents.

A few years ago the president of a Midwestern institution was in New England on a wintry night, trying to find the home of a man who had previously made gifts to his prairie college. Lost in the storm, he finally knocked at a door to ask directions. The man who opened the door insisted upon his coming in and warming himself by the open fire. They introduced themselves and the conversation led to a mutual friendship. Before the president left that night he had told the purpose of his visit to the town, and his host was deeply impressed by the man's evident devotion. Soon he, too, was a contributing friend of the college, and before long made a gift of $200,000 to establish a professorship there.

Dwight L. Moody was the same indefatigable money raiser for humanitarian enterprises of his day that Benjamin Franklin had been a hundred-odd years earlier. Moody, who would have been one of the great nineteenth-century captains of industry had he pursued a business career, would start out with breathless energy to solicit funds for any good cause in which he became interested. Going confidently to men's offices and homes, he begged for their money as directly as he "begged for their conversion" in his religious meetings.

In 1867, when he was a rising young businessman in Chicago, the Y.M.C.A., of which he was an official, caught fire. When he saw that the building was doomed, he dashed out to solicit funds to rebuild it. He rallied other directors and together they went to the merchants with the appeal: "Our hall is burning, sir, the engines are at work but there is no hope. We shall need a new one. Let us have money to begin at once." Thousands of dollars were subscribed immediately, and it is said that Moody and his fellow directors raised enough to build a larger Y.M.C.A. even before the fire was extinguished.

How Dr. X Obtained a Big Subscription

A few years ago the Reverend Dr. X, who was engaged in building a great edifice to house his church in New York, dropped in to see me and asked if I would accompany him on a visit to a wealthy member of his religious denomination (Mr. Y), from whom he hoped to get a gift of half a million dollars to complete the building. Since I was not personally acquainted with Mr. Y, I demurred. But Dr. X pleaded with me so earnestly, on the grounds that he needed the moral support of a friend in making his solicitation, that I agreed to go along.

We were ushered into a beautiful air-cooled, mahogany-furnished office. After the introduction I expected Dr. X to begin his plea. There was not long to wait, but I confess I was startled by the manner in which he proceeded. Without preliminaries he said to Mr. Y:

"May we bow and have a word of prayer?"

Mr. Y assented and he and I bowed our heads while Dr. X dropped to his knees. He then proceeded to pray fervently to the Lord "that this fine Christian man might be moved in heart and mind to give me half a million dollars for the completion of this house of worship which I am trying to build to the glory of Thy name." His prayer went on for several minutes, and in his supplication Dr. X rehearsed all the reasons why Mr. Y should give $500,000 to His cause. Not once did he address his appeal directly to the man himself.

When the prayer was over he arose and we assumed attitudes of expectancy. I confess I was considerably taken aback, even embarrassed. But I need not have been, for shortly Mr. Y stated that he *would* give the half million dollars needed, and in a few moments the visit ended with mutual protestations of gratitude, appreciation, and good will.

It was one of the strangest solicitations I have ever witnessed.

A TENDER HEART IN A ROUGH EXTERIOR

Some years ago when a laymen's committee—headed by Will H. Hays as chairman and Andrew W. Mellon as treasurer—was raising fifteen million dollars to establish a pension system for Presbyterian ministers, we sent a man whom I shall call Mr. Nesbit to ask a businessman in a Midwestern city (Mr. Z) to take an active part in the program. Mr. Z had the reputation of attending his church only on Easter and Christmas, and also of being the most profane (as well as the richest) man in his city.

Mr. Z listened for a few moments and then, instead of exploding as had been expected, he asked, "Did you say your name is Nesbit?"

"Yes," replied the visitor.

"Nesbit, Nesbit," mused Mr. Z. "It was the name of the old Presbyterian pastor of my sainted mother. She often said that he gave his all—his whole life—to the people in his church and laid up nothing for his old age. Nesbit, Nesbit—my lovely, beloved mother."

Then he turned on his visitor roughly and cried, "Go tell Will Hays and Andy Mellon I'll give $100,000 to their ———, ——— pension fund, and they were ——— lucky, or smart—I don't know which—to send a man with your name to see me."

Of course, it was pure chance—or Providence, as you will— for Mr. Z's mother had been dead these many years and the Reverend Mr. Nesbit was not even a memory in the minds of those who keep the earthly rolls of the General Assembly.

TIMES HAVE CHANGED

The increasing complexity of modern life makes it more and more difficult for a financial agent to function effectively, at least without the assistance of modern public relations techniques. It is often impossible for him even to get access to the offices or homes of many of those whom he wishes to visit. If he does succeed in meeting his prospect, he is apt to find his cause in direct competition with a great array of other humanitarian appeals already on the donor's list of benevolences. Because so much time and effort are consumed in trying unsuccessfully to secure interviews, this method of raising funds is now costly.

It has become necessary in recent years for colleges to appoint full-time assistants, with the sole duty of raising funds. No longer called financial agent, their present title may be vice-president, assistant to the president, public relations director, or development director.

A MODERN DEVELOPMENT PROGRAM

Their duties are more complicated—and capable of being much more productive—than those of the old-time financial agent who, single-handed, visited individuals and solicited them one by one. Today, a fund-raising program involves many activities, all co-ordinated in a well-conceived, long-range endeavor to make friends and to win support. The modern independent college, for instance, will do well to establish a *development department*, with a competent, full-time administrator in charge. Under his general direction will operate the annual alumni fund for current scholarship and other operating support, the publicity and public relations activities, a continuous stimulation of bequests for general endowments, a carefully planned approach to foundations and corporations for special grants, and—once in every five to ten years—an intensive, well-organized campaign, directed at all friends of the college, for capital gifts for new buildings.

AN INTENSIVE CAMPAIGN

This periodic intensive campaign acts as the harvest period for bringing in capital gifts from all the friends of the institution who have been cultivated over the previous years. Not only is the intensive campaign an essential harvesting technique; it also serves to locate many new friends, as well as to stimulate new interest in old friends. The constituency of a philanthropic institution is never static. Friends of old pass on and new friends must be found to take their places. Consequently, the college or hospital which ventures an intensive fund-raising effort for capital needs only once in a quarter century misses the support of many others who in the interim would have helped generously and gladly had well-organized approaches been made.

A recent experience by Davidson College in North Carolina is of interest in this connection. For over twenty years Davidson had avoided any intensive campaign for funds and, consequently, had developed need for several new buildings. In 1939 Dr. John R. Cunningham, newly installed president, recommended a campaign for $250,000 for a new gymnasium. The trustees acquiesced and the dreaded campaign proceeded. Instead of anticipated unpleasantness, it turned into a happy affair in which alumni and other friends worked enthusiastically and gave generously. Six years later President Cunningham, buoyed up by the previous success, dared to launch another campaign—this time for $2,500,-000—and this also turned out to be a complete success both in money and spirit.

STIMULATION OF BEQUESTS

The intensive campaign, however, is seldom able to obtain substantial additions to endowment. Its greatest usefulness is in gathering capital funds for new buildings. Endowments come, for the most part, through bequests from deceased friends rather than from outright gifts from living friends. I estimate that 90 percent of the endowments of all of our philanthropic institutions have come through bequests. This custom is one of the traditions of American giving.

Since this is so, it is important for a college or other philanthropic institution to give careful attention year by year to reminding its friends to remember the institution in their wills. Such stimulation, carefully planned and sincerely applied, brings results. It is amazing to follow the constant flow of charitable bequests in this nation day by day—most of it for permanent endowments. And it is most interesting to seek the reason and the occasion for the bequest, which often reach back far beyond the knowledge of those now in charge of the institution. In one such instance a college recently received word of a bequest of $10,000 from the estate of a lady in her eighties, of whom no one presently at the college had ever heard. On investigation it developed that seventy-five years before, this lady's parents had entertained the president of the college in their home over Sunday when he, a Baptist minister, was to preach in their little church. The college president had been kind to the little girl and had so impressed her that seventy-five years later she left this bequest to the college he had represented and which she herself had never even seen.

Recently two wealthy persons died and the newspapers published the facts in regard to their estates. One—Mrs. Matthew Astor Wilks—was reported to have left an estate of $95,000,000, out of which she had bequeathed $87,000,000 to sixty-three different educational, religious, and philanthropic institutions. Because of these philanthropic bequests, her estate taxes were reduced to a minimum and vast sums were invested by Mrs. Wilks in permanent service to oncoming generations.

About the same time the papers reported that the estate of a man recently deceased had totaled $75,000,000, but that since he had not made any notable philanthropic bequests, the estate taxes would take $56,000,000. I wonder why such a man, who disliked the extravagant spending of our Federal Government, had failed to leave great sums to certain institutions which he had supported generously during his life, rather than leave the bulk of his estate to be absorbed by general governmental expenditures.

UNITED NEGRO COLLEGE FUND

A significant development within the past ten years has been the creation of the United Negro College Fund, a federated fund-raising program of 31 accredited private Negro Colleges. Dr. Frederick D. Patterson, president of the Fund, says of it, "The success of this cooperative movement has demonstrated that many of our citizens will give to a broad and objective view of education in which the needs of youth provide the basis." The United Negro College Fund raises about $1,500,000 each year which is pro-rated to the member colleges for operating expenses, and is now also engaged in raising a capital fund of $25,000,000 for non-recurring building and equipment needs.

THE COLLEGE PRESIDENT AS A FUND RAISER

Although the modern college president is no longer the "financial agent" in the same sense that his earlier predecessor was, nevertheless he is still the key figure in the most vital aspects of a college's fund-raising program. No matter how efficient any assistant delegated to this task may prove to be, there comes a time when only the president can successfully close the appeal for a large gift. He is the man whom the large donor quite rightly wants to see. In certain interviews he—and he alone—*is* the college and unless he is willing to function thus in fund raising, his college will probably miss important opportunities to obtain substantial gifts.

In the recent past there grew up a cult in some of our educational circles which caricatured the college president as a Babbitt go-getter and sought to ridicule his fund-raising function. As a consequence, some colleges have had to assure their prospective presidents that they would not have to raise funds; that this would be done by the trustees and others.

Alas, these assurances are not long valid for the college president completely dedicated to his task; he soon discovers that the growing needs of his institution must be met with more funds, and that he alone must provide the top leadership in such a program.

I well recall two great college and university presidents of our day who turned to fund raising with a will and a zest, even though their contracts specifically excused them from this duty.

In 1929 Dr. Franklin W. Johnson, then at the age of 59, was about to retire from a distinguished career on the faculty of Teachers College in New York. When the trustees of his Alma Mater—Colby College—elected him their president, Dr. Johnson demurred, saying he was neither an administrator nor a fund raiser. The trustees promptly wrote into his contract a clause excusing him from fund raising. Only a year after taking office he discovered, as a result of a survey of the higher educational institutions of Maine, that Colby College would be obliged to give up its 120-year-old site within the city of Waterville if it were to modernize its educational plant, and that it would have to build an entirely new plant on a new campus three miles away.

The new president smiled wryly and tore up his non-fund-raising contract. For the next twenty years—even after he became president emeritus—he gave brilliant and devoted leadership to raising a fund of many millions of dollars for the new campus on Mayflower Hill. Said he, when the last new building was completed and occupied in the fall of 1952, "I have seen my heart's desire!"

Another educator, who voluntarily abrogated a non-fund-raising clause in his contract was the late Dr. Edmund Ezra Day, president and chancellor of Cornell University. In 1948 he and the trustees launched a capital-fund-raising program for twelve and a half million dollars. When he learned that he would be expected to give the major part of his time for two years to that endeavor, he asked blandly, "What about that clause in my contract that says I'll have no responsibility for fund raising?" The answer was, "Let your conscience be your guide." He grinned and went to work at the new task so energetically and zestfully that near the close of the successful effort he confided to his campaign director: "I'm glad you made me do it. I've had the time of my life. I never realized that fund raising was such fun!"

I recall another college president whose reaction to his success in fund raising was slightly different—he being of the younger generation of intellectuals who have been taught to disdain money and all efforts to obtain it. The college of which he is president had for years needed money for a new building but had done nothing about it, resting upon the naïve assumption that it needed only to be a good college to attract money as a natural result.

Having tested this assumption for some years and receiving no such manna, this president undertook a fund-raising campaign, after much reluctance and protestation. He did his part splendidly; in due time the entire fund was raised and the building erected and dedicated. He received many words of praise from the friends of the college—so many, in fact, that he confided to his campaign director: "I'm beginning to be sorry that we had such a success." When asked why, he replied, "Because I'm afraid from now on I'll be known as one of these ——— fund-raising college presidents instead of as an educator."

CHAPTER X

The Creation of the Financial Campaign

TO THE human science and art of fund raising for philanthropic causes, one can well apply the wisdom of the classic couplet:

> The old order changeth—giving place to new—
> Lest one good custom should corrupt the world.

In the twentieth century, Americans have learned habits of giving which have resulted in a phenomenal rise in the volume and the number of their voluntary gifts to philanthropic causes.

The figures speak for themselves. In 1900 we gave to all the colleges in the land a total of $11,995,000; today, gifts to independent colleges are about $300,000,000 a year—an increase during this half century of 2,500 per cent. The philanthropic gifts of the American people to all causes totaled about $500,000,000 in 1900, while this last year, in 1952, they were well over four billion dollars. This was an increase out of all proportion to the increase in population and wealth. Judged by any comparison with these factors, *giving has increased abnormally*. Other explanations must be sought for our modern habits of increasingly widespread and generous benefactions.

The most important single factor in the amazing increase in giving during the twentieth century *was the creation of a new technique for inducing people to give*. Though now familiar to nearly everyone, it came as a brand-new idea. It was created by two young men—Lyman L. Pierce and Charles S. Ward—thinking and working indepedently at first, but later joining their efforts to evolve what is commonly known as the "financial campaign."

These two men were both Y.M.C.A. secretaries. Lyman Pierce, a native of western New York State, after graduating from the University of Minnesota, at once went into Y.M.C.A. work, his first job being financial and membership secretary at Omaha. Being a young man of superior ideals and spiritual capacities, he was greatly disturbed because his time was being devoted almost entirely to financial efforts necessary to keep the work alive. Far from accepting this situation, he began to work out a plan by which he could compress his membership and fund-raising tasks into a brief space of time, and thus free himself during the balance of the year for character-building work among the young men of the community.

In 1890 he enlisted a hundred of the leading men of Omaha in a membership campaign—each man to get one new member a month, until the total membership should reach 1,500. These hundred men were divided into twenty teams. Printed matter was prepared and regular report meetings held. It was a great success—and lots of fun as well. News of the new method spread quickly throughout the entire "Y." Thus was born the modern, intensive, organized campaign which has brought billions of dollars of increased giving to the philanthropies of America.

Charles S. Ward, born in Vermont and educated at Dartmouth, also entered the service of the Y.M.C.A. when he came out of college. In 1897 he was general secretary at Grand Rapids. He persuaded his directors to agree to close down their own business desks for a month and to see so many people each day in quest of subscriptions for the work of the Y. He promised that if they would do this there would need to be nothing more said or done the rest of the year about finances.

The newspapers told of this novel undertaking—*spectacular,* it was termed in those days—and the whole city watched with intense interest. The eleven-month recess from financial solicitation proved a happy experience for the directors. It also proved so interesting to the rest of the Association brotherhood that Charles Ward was soon called to New York as financial secretary of the International Committee of the Y.M.C.A. He was sent from city to city to tell other local associations of his experience at Grand Rapids and to help them put similar plans into operation.

Meanwhile, in 1900, Lyman Pierce had been called to the general secretaryship of the Y in Washington, D.C. With his restless energy he brought about an extension of the program in that city and gradually persuaded his directors to undertake a new building, to cost the unprecedented sum of $300,000. In 1905 he sent to the International Committee to obtain the help of Ward in the direction of a campaign for that amount. Here, the paths of the two men met. Merging their ideas and experience, they evolved the modern "whirlwind" campaign. It was Pierce who made the bold suggestion that the campaign be cut down to *a week's time* and that, in order to accomplish this result, a larger number of volunteer solicitors be enlisted. *Mirabile dictu*— it worked.

Following the Washington experience Ward adopted the plans worked out there as his standard practice. From that time on he went about the nation directing similar Y.M.C.A. building campaigns in scores of cities. The greatest of these efforts occurred in New York City in 1913, when the Y.M.C.A. and the Y.W.C.A. jointly determined to raise four million dollars for needed new buildings. This announcement took people's breath away. No single event in the field of philanthropy had ever been of so spectacular a nature as that unbelievable proposal to raise four millions in ten days. But the campaign was a success. A total of $4,095,000 was contributed by 17,400 people, 400 of the contributors—including the John D. Rockefellers, father and son— giving $3,600,000 in large amounts, while 17,000 others followed their lead with smaller contributions totaling $495,000.

This and other similar achievements of the campaign method now began to attract the attention of hospitals, colleges, and various welfare societies. Charles Ward was in great demand, and almost everywhere he went an amazing success resulted.

Meanwhile, Lyman Pierce had been called to Australia and New Zealand as national secretary of the Y.M.C.A., and for three years he went from one city to another, using the American method of financing buildings. On his return he spent a year traveling over the United States as a field secretary of the Laymen's Missionary Movement, and in this capacity gave instruction and inspiration to the leaders of the Protestant denominations in the new technique of raising philanthropic funds. The intensive campaign method was soon adopted by many local churches in what was called the Every-Member Canvass and, as a consequence, giving to Protestant churches experienced a sharp rise.

It was in 1913 that the first college used, effectively, the new campaign method as a means of raising capital funds. This was the University of Pittsburgh, then in transition from the old Western University of Pennsylvania, whose campus was being moved from Allegheny to the Schenley Park region. Charles Ward was again generously loaned by the National Council to direct the campaign. By strange coincidence, Lyman Pierce was then general secretary of the Pittsburgh Y.M.C.A., so he also sat in on the plans.

Immediately after World War I—when great additions to plant and endowment were everywhere needed, because of postponed building programs and increased enrollments—literally hundreds of colleges organized intensive campaigns. Similarly, thousands of hospitals and welfare and religious organizations planned the raising of substantial capital funds in the same manner. The Community Chest idea had also grown out of the experience in World War I, and hundreds of community chests were established throughout America in that same period. They made similar use of the intensive campaign technique.

As a consequence there was a great demand for experienced campaign directors. Immediately after the war several of the nationally known firms of professional fund-raising counsel had their beginnings. Pierce and Ward, who had directed the great war fund campaigns of 1917 and 1918—such as the Red Cross, the Y.M.C.A., and United War Work—formed, together with five associates, one of the early firms in 1919. Five of the present outstanding firms in the fund-raising field developed as offshoots of this original group, called Ward, Hill, Pierce and Wells.

CHAPTER XI

The Rise of a New Profession

THE upsurge of philanthropic giving in America, which we have been noting, may be attributed to several causes. Chief among them are three: the increase in American wealth and income, the creation of new campaign techniques, and the rise of a new profession—that of *fund raising*. The spectacular rise in giving in the past ten years from two and a half billion dollars to over four billion dollars a year is due especially to the campaign method just described, and to the growing skill, numbers, and efficiency of the nation's professional fund raisers.

This term used to have—and with some still has—an uncomplimentary flavor. It implied a person who would do almost anything to wheedle or trick a few dollars out of the public for any so-called "charity." Unfortunately, there were some such persons, and still are. But during the past generation there has been developing a more dignified profession. It is composed of men and women who are bringing tested experience, character, and dedication to the work of helping philanthropic agencies present their legitimate claims.

1. STAFF MEMBERS

These professional fund raisers may be divided roughly into two groups: *first,* those employed on the permanent staffs of colleges, hospitals, and various social agencies to give their full time to raising funds for their respective institutions. Already there are probably five thousand or more such men and women. In addition, there are several thousand other staff members who give a large part of their time to fund raising and the balance to related duties, such as public relations.

As yet, there is no recognized system of professional education for fund raisers; as a result, the training of these men and women is limited. Also, the turnover is still too rapid to provide the

112

majority of them with a solid background of experience in the various phases of the task. Certain segments, however, have already created their own professional organizations. The rapid growth of this group of staff members is illustrated by the recent development of the American College Public Relations Association, started on a modest scale in 1927 by T. T. Frankenberg of Columbus, Ohio, a public relations consultant. At first called the American Association of College News Bureaus, its membership included only the paid publicity directors of the colleges. There were then probably less than a hundred such full-time directors. Today, this public relations association has over 800 members.

There are now undoubtedly a thousand colleges and universities with permanent fund-raising staff members. Some of the larger universities have considered the work so important that they have appointed vice-presidents for fund-raising duties; others have given such staff members a designation as director of public relations or development. Whatever the title, the related duties of public relations and fund raising have become recognized as an essential and important staff function in the modern university or large college. The fund-raising and development staff of one university, which has been successful in this field, has a total of forty employees, including both executives and clerks.

Certainly the numbers, skill, and prestige of professional fund raisers on the staffs of permanent institutions is on the rise, and it is to be hoped that an increasing number of them will stay on their fund-raising jobs long enough to get far beyond the trial-and-error stage of competence.

2. COUNSELORS AND CAMPAIGN DIRECTORS

The *second* group of professional fund raisers is that of men who are employed on the staffs of fund-raising firms. There are a score or more of such firms, with experienced staffs totaling perhaps a thousand men—many of whom are outstanding in their ability to plan and direct a specific campaign for funds. Further, there are several hundred more men and women outside these concerns who operate independently as free lances in fund-raising and public relations counseling.

Several years ago it appeared to the officers of some of the well-

established firms centering in New York that they had a responsibility for taking the lead in setting standards for the new
profession they were helping to create. In consequence, they
initiated a movement to organize such an association. The proposed group came into being in 1935 as the American Association of Fund-Raising Counsel. It has proved to be an important
factor both in the rise of this new profession and in public understanding of its aims and methods. The following paragraphs from
a published statement of the Association's purposes give valuable
sidelights on our whole question:

FOR YOUR SERVICE AND PROTECTION

Whenever a special skill becomes essential for the fulfillment of some
needed social function a profession grows up to meet the need, and
this has been true in the field of Fund-Raising, as it was previously true
in the fields of Journalism and Advertising. . . .

*Fund-Raising as a profession grew out of the interest of men and
women in the advancement of philanthropy.* Pioneers came largely
from the fields of education, health, welfare, religion and civic enterprise. These pioneers were persons who had been responsible for raising
funds for the regular maintenance of philanthropic organizations and
saw an opportunity for wider service by bringing their experience to
bear in furthering scientific methods in fund-raising. In the past quarter-
century the fields of Journalism, Public Relations and Law have also
provided recruits to the profession. What is more important is that
today there are many men who have known no other career but have
chosen fund-raising as their profession and trained for it from their
college days.

FOUNDING OF THE ASSOCIATION

In the year 1935 nine firms recognized as leaders of the profession
joined together to form the American Association of Fund-Raising
Counsel for the promotion of certain objectives directly concerned
with improving the technique of fund-raising service—objectives in-
herently sound and necessary if the public is to be well served.

It is obviously of the utmost importance to the future well-being of
our American religious, educational and social agencies that the efforts

to raise funds in their behalf be conducted in the most honorable and effective manner possible. The purpose of the Association is to contribute to this end. . . .

STANDARDS OF THE PROFESSION

The by-laws of the Association set forth the qualifications for membership, and the standards of professional ethics and practice to which its members are committed are as follows:

That the active executive head of a member organization shall have had a continuous experience of at least ten years as professional counsel in the fund-raising field.

That the member organization must have a record of consistently successful work and of repeated calls to serve the same clients, or others involving the same constituency.

That they must furnish satisfactory references, both from clients and from one or more banks or trust companies.

That they must conform to the minimum standards of assigning as executives-in-charge, or campaign directors, only those members of their staffs who have served as associates on six or more campaigns, or who have been continuously employed as staff members for a period of at least one year.

That membership in the Association be limited to those organizations which do business on a fixed-fee basis only (not on a percentage basis) and make no profit, directly or indirectly, from disbursements for the accounts of clients.

RESPONSIBILITIES OF THE PROFESSION

Conforming to these standards, the member firms all maintain permanent staffs of trained directors and associate directors, and provide for training periods for new personnel in the expectation that such staff additions will also be permanent. It is not the policy of member firms to seek staff expansion on a temporary basis.

Supervision by the firm's officers or partners during campaigns is a regular part of their service to clients; and, in seeking new business, an officer or partner of the firm visits the client and makes a careful study of the case before a contract is signed.

One of the major responsibilities of fund-raising counsel is to budget and administer funds covering the necessary expenses of all fund-raising efforts, in addition to the fee paid to professional counsel. These expenses cover such items as office rent, printing, postage, meetings, clerical and secretarial assistance, telephone, telegraph, supplies, multigraphing and mimeographing, travel and living expenses. . . .

Because of these and other self-imposed standards, the American Association of Fund-Raising Counsel assures the client of capable campaign direction, of a service conforming to a strict code of ethical practice, and of what experience has proved to be the most effective and economical procedure for the raising of funds.

MEMBERS OF THE A.A.F.R.C.

Aderton-Johnson Associates	Harrisburg, Pa.
American City Bureau	Chicago, Ill.
Beaver Associates, Inc.	Chicago, Ill.
Reuel Estill & Co., Inc.	New York, N.Y.
Charles W. Gamble & Associates	New York, N.Y.
John Price Jones Co., Inc.	New York, N.Y.
Kersting, Brown & Co., Inc.	New York, N.Y.
Ketchum, Inc.	Pittsburgh, Pa.
Marts and Lundy, Inc.	New York, N.Y.
Pierce, Hedrick and Sherwood, Inc.	New York, N.Y.
Tamblyn and Brown, Inc.	New York, N.Y.
Ward, Wells, Dreshman & Reinhardt	New York, N.Y.
Will, Folsom and Smith, Inc.	New York, N.Y.

A FUND RAISER SPEAKS

At a recent session of the Work-Shop on Public Relations and Fund Raising of the Conference on Administration of Church-Related Schools, held at Green Lake, Wisconsin, Louis W. Robey, vice-president of one of the member firms of the A.A.F.R.C., described the profession in an address from which we quote some excerpts. These few paragraphs will give the reader some indication of the rising sense of dignity and social usefulness which is coming to permeate our present-day professional fund raisers:

Would you like to engage in a profession which is interesting because it consists of creative work with human beings; which is challenging because it deals with basic—and sometimes seemingly impossible —problems which *must* be solved; and which is satisfying because it performs a great part in helping this confused world of ours get itself straightened out? Well, if you would, just stay where you are, because you are in it. . . .

And let us see clearly that this is intellectual work of a high order. We are very much inclined to think of intellectual work only in the so-called "pure" field—pure mathematics, or pure science, or pure literature. We are inclined to think that the solution of a practical problem is of a somewhat lower order, whereas the two are really exactly the same, except in different fields. The same amount of ability to analyze and to form a judgment is required of both.

One is of just as high a type as the other. One concerns applied scholarship and the other abstract scholarship. We don't always recognize this because, as the late Dr. John Erskine of Columbia University once said: "Whenever scholarship is applied with success to the amelioration of life, it risks the reputation of being tarnished. It is no longer pure." Dean Willard Sperry has expressed the same idea in another way. "A general assumption seems to be abroad," he says in his book *Religion in America*, "that the sons of Mary are somehow superior to the sons of Martha."

Fund-raisers are the sons of Martha using the same kind of creative and inventive intelligence as the sons of Mary.

> "All the means of action—
> The shapeless mass, the materials—
> Lie everywhere about us. What we need
> Is the celestial fire to change the flint
> Into transparent crystal, bright and clear.
>   That fire is genius."

Some call it art. . . .

I have just one more thing to say. That is, that the rewards of public relations and fund-raising are supremely satisfying. Let us remember that the ultimate result of what we do is the building of manhood and womanhood for the future; that we do this by the exercise of the highest powers given to man, namely, his creative and inventive intelligence; that to do this, we have to guide, influence and direct keen human personalities; and that, were it not for us, a great gap would be left in the forces of this world fighting for its betterment. When we remember all these things, we ought to be superlatively happy in the work we are trying to do.

It cannot yet be claimed that the practice of fund raising as a full-time occupation has become a fully recognized profession. It has still to attain that status in the public mind. However, it is gaining in dignity and in recognition as dedicated and capable men and women give themselves, full time, to this occupation as a career. Those who devote their lives to its practice discover that there emerge basic principles which can be applied in a variety of situations, and that long experience clearly classifies certain methods and measures as proper and effective, and other methods as illusory and wasteful. It is depressing to observe how some fund raisers continue to try methods which the experienced practitioners have long since learned are not effective.

Fund raising as a skill or art or profession may be still in its youth, but it is growing up. Whenever a college or other privately supported agency takes fund raising seriously and plans for it as an essential and dignified phase of its permanent administrative job, it can obtain experienced and competent counsel adequate for its needs. Such employment of counsel is steadily increasing.

In a recent address at the New York School of Social Work, Dr. Charles Dollard, president of Carnegie Corporation, spoke of the recent developments of a new profession—that of social work —in words that are pertinent in the consideration of fund raising as a profession:

The pressure to transform an occupation or vocation into a profession arises naturally from within any group of practitioners whose work involves extensive preparation or apprenticeship. They have a natural interest in establishing standards of character, training, and performance, which will raise barriers against the incompetent, and increase the status and the rewards of their calling. While this pressure towards professionalism might in one sense be labeled selfish, the results are beneficent for society as a whole. Professionalizing any activity tends to institutionalize the best ways of doing the job, and to create standards of quality which serve the public interest.

Today the social worker is much farther along in his progress toward a professional career than is the fund raiser, as degree-granting schools of social work have been established. It is to be hoped that the practice of fund raising as a full-time career will attract more and more men and women who will, in time, bring it up to the status of a profession of well-recognized standing.

PART FIVE

How Do High Taxes Affect Giving?

CHAPTER XII

Have Taxes Killed the Goose That Laid the Golden Eggs?

T HE answer is No.

Shortly after the revolutionary "first hundred days" of the New Deal in 1933, President Franklin D. Roosevelt and his advisers revealed their plans to lay upon the nation great new levies of *taxation*. The Federal Government was to assume entirely new responsibilities for the welfare of people in emergent need. At this news many educational and philanthropic leaders feared they saw an end to large-scale *giving* in America. They sounded an alarm which, in my opinion, has been proved a false one, but which still reverberates. The distinguished president of one of the nation's leading universities said to his alumni—inadvisedly, it now appears:

In the history of the University we have arrived at the end of an era during which most generous and great gifts were received from many different individuals for the endowment and enrichment of the work of the University. . . . The great fortunes and the large accumulations which made these benefactions possible are either dissipated or destroyed. . . .

Should these great fortunes be renewed—either in whole or in part—an extravagant government stands ready to take a great proportion of their annual income in taxation. . . . A steady flow of gifts from the alumni—moderate in amount but large in number—must be one of the University's chief sources of dependence for its continued usefulness in the years that lie just ahead of us.

MANY GLOOMY PROPHETS

This prophecy was picked up and repeated by other philanthropic leaders. The head of the most powerful board of a great religious denomination said:

It would seem that the day of large gifts may be over. If income and inheritance taxes absorb the wealth which has been available in the past, then the loss must be made up by the larger number of small givers.

A little later a conference of several hundred presidents and trustees of colleges and universities went on record with this gloomy prediction:

There will be fewer men giving millions of dollars to this or that institution. This seems to be clearly proven by the evidence of the last three or four years; hence, the college which is going to grow and develop in answering the social needs of the future must look about for new means of support.

Opposition political leaders latterly picked this up as an issue and one of them published a full-page advertisement in a metropolitan newspaper, entitled "Destructive Taxes Will Eventually Cripple College, Church and Charity." This was a public reply to a letter which he had received from a college president soliciting a gift. In the advertisement he said:

All responsible heads of institutions writing letters similar to that which you address to me should—as a matter of duty to the institution represented, as well as decorum to the person solicited—express their abhorrence of a system of taxation (government) that destroys initiative, invites governmental extravagance, involves ever-increasing taxation, lays the groundwork for a totalitarian state, and sounds the death knell of the very work in which they are engaged. . . .

During the last twenty years, the masses—led by the radical press and by swarms of vociferous politicians, pulpiteers and professors—have been more than advocating the crippling—they are demanding the destruction—of that element whose ingenuity, initiative, progressiveness and aggressiveness made us a great nation.

This destruction can be accomplished by any one of three methods: by wholesale murder, by confiscation of capital, or by high and discriminatory taxes. The latter method has been chosen in our country, although it may take two generations to accomplish that which could be done in a day by either of the other methods. . . . When the goose is killed, it stops laying golden eggs. When the seed corn is destroyed there can be no crop.

Therefore, unless men like you who head educational institutions—in conjunction with those interested in hospitals, the Y.M.C.A. and the Red Cross—sponsor a movement and make it a successful movement to prevent a continuation of the improper use of the power of taxation, and substitute reasonable taxation—equitable taxation, general taxation, in place of punitive taxation—then let me tell you that you are on your last round-up. The future solicitor will be compelled to make his appeal for dollar-and-dime contributions!

The fear of "no more large giving" spread like wildfire after 1933; I have in my files literally scores of published reiterations of this prediction repeated time and again during the past twenty years—chiefly by college presidents. A pronouncement from one well-known person forecast that because of the "drying-up of philanthropy due to taxes, 500 colleges would soon close their doors." (In Chapter XVI you will read that there are now 450 *more* colleges than there were in 1934!)

This prophecy of the end of generous giving was, in my opinion, one of the greatest errors made by philanthropic leaders in our lifetime.

The forecasts sounded plausible and many people believed them. So many have repeated them that they have become a cliché which is expected in every statement on philanthropic giving—especially in general appeals for *more* gifts. Even one of the most generous philanthropists of our generation made use of this trite phrase, in December, 1952, in his testimony before a congressional committee, when he told the committee that philanthropic institutions cannot depend much longer on large family fortunes to finance their work, as income and estate taxes will absorb all the money which used to be available for philanthropy.

The only trouble with this plausible alarm is that it has proved to be not so. It is true that income taxes are incredibly high, but the actual facts of the matter are that there are more wealthy men and women in the high-income brackets now than there were in the "golden 1920's," and that in spite of high income taxes, they are giving more to philanthropy now than in the twenties—both in amounts and in percentages. In theory, the alarms sound plausible and true: in fact, they are proving false.

Following are facts taken from the published reprints of the Internal Revenue Bureau of the U.S. Treasury Department. I have made a comparison of income and contributions of income recipients in the highest brackets, between the 1920 decade and the latest four years (1947, 1948, 1949, and 1950) for which published reports are available.

INCOMES OF $500,000 AND OVER

Period	Number of Taxpayers	Total Income	Total Contributions	Contribution Equal to % Income
1922-29	747	$999,526,000	$34,998,000	.035
1947	416	416,757,000	33,126,000	.08
1948	564	532,776,000	39,584,000	.07
1949	497	509,852,000	38,731,000	.075
1950	842	852,869,000	55,142,000	.064

In 1947 income was 42% of 1922-29 but contributions were 94.4%
In 1948 income was 53% of 1922-29 but contributions were 113.1%
In 1949 income was 51% of 1922-29 but contributions were 101.9%
In 1950 income was 85% of 1922-29 but contributions were 129.1%

INCOMES OF $150,000 TO $500,000

Period	Number of Taxpayers	Total Income	Total Contributions	Contribution Equal to % Income
1922-29	4,158	$1,162,961,000	$31,533,000	.027
1947	4,075	927,255,000	51,464,000	.055
1948	6,097	1,371,034,000	66,410,000	.048
1949	5,192	1,184,396,000	64,788,000	.054
1950	19,547	3,204,545,000	129,054,000	.04

In 1947 income was 80 % of 1922-29 but contributions were 163.0%
In 1948 income was 117 % of 1922-29 but contributions were 210.0%
In 1949 income was 101.9% of 1922-29 but contributions were 205.4%
In 1950 income was 275.5% of 1922-29 but contributions were 409.2%

INCOMES OF $50,000 TO $150,000

Period	Number of Taxpayers	Total Income	Total Contributions	Contribution Equal to % Income
1922-29	23,919	$2,169,592,000	$ 53,240,000	.024
1947	44,402	3,285,690,000	124,620,000	.038
1948	62,344	4,669,538,000	142,600,000	.030
1949	54,158	4,035,230,000	134,920,000	.038
1950	62,689	4,192,517,000	113,894,000	.027

In 1947 income was 151.4% of 1922-29 but contributions were 234%
In 1948 income was 210.0% of 1922-29 but contributions were 267%
In 1949 income was 185.9% of 1922-29 but contributions were 234%
In 1950 income was 193.2% of 1922-29, but contributions were 213.8%

Let us now draw from the following summary our conclusions as to the validity of the pessimistic prophesies which we reviewed at the beginning of this chapter.

ALL INCOMES OVER $50,000 PER YEAR

Period	Number of Taxpayers	Total Income	Total Contributions	Contribution Equal to % Income
1922-29	28,824	$4,332,079,000	$119,771,000	.028
1950	83,078	8,249,931,000	298,090,000	.036

What is *your* conclusion?

RECENT BIG GIFTS

As further evidence against this "end of an era of philanthropy" cliché, I would like to present the following list of gifts and bequests of $1,000,000 and over, which were publicly announced during the past six years in the New York newspapers. All of these were from individuals, none from foundations. It is quite likely that a great many others were made in the period which were not announced in the New York papers. It is an imposing and inspiring list, which seems to me to indicate, at least, that the alarm was false—that the goose of the golden eggs has not expired:

1947

Amount	From	To
$ 1,000,000	Mr. and Mrs. Will F. Clayton of Houston, Tex.	Johns Hopkins Hospital
7,000,000	Mr. C. Howard Candler of Atlanta, Ga.	Emory University
1,000,000	John DeFerrari, an immigrant fruit peddler	Boston Public Library
2,500,000	S. E. Summerfield of Santa Monica, Calif.	S. E. Summerfield Foundation
1,000,000	Dr. William R. Lovelace of Albuquerque, N.M.	Lovelace Foundation
1,000,000	John B. Gribbel	Hospital in Media, Pa.
1,700,000	Harry S. Wherrett of Pittsburgh, Pa.	Pittsburgh Foundation
2,000,000	C. S. Weston of Scranton, Pa.	Several colleges and philanthropic institutions
7,500,000	Mr. and Mrs. H. E. Manville	Hiram Edward Manville Foundation
33,000,000	Callaway Mills of LaGrange, Ga.	Callaway Community Foundation
1,000,000	Mr. and Mrs. Robert S. Barrett of Alexandria, Va.	The Barrett Foundation
1,000,000	Mrs. Mary D. Faulkner of Woodstock, Vt.	Mary Hitchcock Memorial Hospital
1,350,000	Ira C. Copley of Aurora, Ill.	Copley Memorial

1947—Continued

Amount	From	To
$ 4,000,000	Mrs. Mary A. Stewart of Washington, D.C.	Hospital For research in cancer
1,000,000	Mrs. Helen J. Hunt of New York	Yale University and six other institutions
1,750,000	Mrs. Hugo F. Urbauer of St. Louis, Mo.	Washington University

1948

50,000,000	Four children of the late Joseph N. Pew of Philadelphia, Pa.	Pew Memorial Foundation
6,400,000	R. K. Mellon, of Pittsburgh, Pa.	Richard King Mellon Foundation
3,075,000	Henry K. S. Williams of San Francisco, Calif.	St. Mary's Free Hospital for Children
9,500,000	Thomas W. Lamont of New York	Several institutions
1,500,000	William H. Ackland	Rollins College; Univ. of North Carolina
1,500,000	Miss Theodora Wilbour of New York	Several Boston Institutions
1,250,000	Mrs. Margaret H. Turrell	Turrell Foundation for Needy Children
2,750,000	Mrs. Marguerite S. Davis of Long Island, N.Y.	Group of philanthropic institutions
2,000,000	Ernest L. Woodward of Leroy, N.Y.	Univ. of Rochester and four other institutions
1,000,000	Crapo C. Smith of Ann Arbor, Mich.	Michigan University
1,000,000	Mary Louise Walker of New York	Methodist Church Home for the Aged
2,000,000	Arthur T. Elting of New York	Phillips Exeter Academy
1,000,000	Frank J. Lewis of Chicago	Loyola University
2,500,000	Mrs. Mabel W. Jones of New York	Village of Lithopolis, Ohio
1,000,000	F. R. Newman of Cleveland	Cornell University
15,000,000	William M. Cromwell of New York	48 philanthropic institutions
40,000,000	Eugene Higgins of New York and Paris	Four universities
1,000,000	Mrs. Josephine Schwed of New York	New York University
5,000,000	Mrs. Mary Fuller Frazier of Philadelphia, Pa.	Village of Perryopolis, Pa.
2,750,000	Major Edward Bowes of New York	St. Patrick's Cathedral

1948—Continued

Amount	From	To
$ 1,000,000	Mrs. Anita McCormick Blaine of Chicago	Foundation for World Government
2,500,000	Mrs. Andrew Carnegie of New York	Several philanthropic institutions
2,400,000	Anonymous donor	Permanent Charity Fund of Boston
2,000,000	Mrs. Henrietta P. Lippincott of New York	St. Thomas Protestant Episcopal Church
1,000,000	"Chinese Christian Business-man"	Presbyterian Board of Foreign Missions
1,150,000	Mrs. Estelle M. Traverso of	Presbyterian Hospital;
2,300,000	New York	United Hospital Fund
1,000,000	Mrs. Florence Troughton of New York	Salvation Army
1,500,000	Myron C. Taylor of New York	Cornell University
1,000,000	C. H. Swift of Chicago	University of Chicago
1,258,000	Mrs. Hugo F. Urbauer of St. Louis, Mo.	Washington University

1949

2,000,000	Allston Burr of Newton, Mass.	Harvard; Great Britain Annuity Fund, etc.
1,750,000	Mr. and Mrs. Alexander W. Weddell, Richmond, Va.	Virginia Historical Society
5,000,000	Mrs. Chauncey D. Clarke of Los Angeles, Calif.	Claremont College
1,300,000	A. Atwater Kent of Philadelphia	Nine universities
2,000,000	John D. Rockefeller, Jr.	National Park in Wyoming
1,500,000	William B. Isham of New York	Princeton University
5,000,000	John D. Rockefeller, Jr.	Harvard University
10,000,000	William S. Eaton of Boston	Eaton Foundation; Many philanthropic institutions
8,000,000	Solomon Guggenheim of New York	S. R. Guggenheim Foundation
1,000,000	Campbell Soup Co. of Camden, N.J.	M.I.T.
5,700,000	Ogden M. Reid of New York	Reid Foundation
1,000,000	Godfrey L. Cabot of Boston	Norwich University
2,000,000	J. Howard Pew of Philadelphia	Institute for Cancer Research
1,000,000	Mrs. Fred J. Fisher of Detroit	University of Notre Dame

1949—Continued

Amount	From	To
$ 1,000,000	Mrs. Keith Spalding of New York	American Museum of Natural History

1950

1,000,000	Mrs. Marion K. McNay of San Antonio, Tex.	San Antonio Art Institute
1,000,000	Ernest M. Morris of South Bend, Ind.	University of Notre Dame
4,000,000	C. A. Frueauff of New York	C. A. Frueauff Foundation
4,000,000	Generoso Pope of New York	Generoso Pope Foundation
1,500,000	I. S. O'Shaughnessy of Golden Beach, Calif.	University of Notre Dame
1,017,000	Ernest G. Stillman of Boston	Harvard University
1,000,000	Dr. Joseph Collins of New York	Joseph Collins Foundation
60,000,000	Mrs. Edward S. Harkness of New York	Commonwealth Fund; Presbyterian Hospital; etc.
4,000,000	Dr. Albert A. Berg of New York	New York University; N.Y. Academy of Medicine; etc.
1,000,000	John Hoober of York, Pa.	Yale University
2,150,000	Jacob R. Schiff of New York	Several charitable institutions
3,000,000	Al Jolson of Hollywood, Calif.	Several charitable institutions
1,000,000	Anonymous donor	Yale University
1,000,000	Frank Z. Atran of New York	Mt. Sinai Hospital
4,000,000	Mrs. Henry Ford	Edison Institute
1,000,000	Charles Newman	Ray Newman Memorial Foundation
5,250,000	Alfred P. Sloan, Jr.	M.I.T.
30,000,000	Julius Rippel of Newark, N.J.	Fannie E. Rippel Foundation

1951

2,800,000	Mrs. Henrietta P. Lippincott of New York	St. Thomas Protestant Episcopal Church
5,000,000	John D. Rockefeller, Jr.	United Negro Colleges Fund
2,000,000	Mr. and Mrs. Walter Arensburg of Hollywood, Calif.	Philadelphia Museum of Art
1,000,000	Sam A. Lewisohn of New York	Six institutions of education and art

1951—Continued

Amount	From	To
$ 1,000,000	George R. Agassiz of Boston	Harvard University
2,000,000	David T. Leahy	Roman Catholic Diocese of Brooklyn
1,000,000	John D. Rockefeller, Jr.	M.I.T.

1952

Amount	From	To
4,200,000	Mrs. Elsie Eckstein of Chicago	Northwestern University
2,000,000	W. A. Haynes of Shreveport, La.	Centenary College
2,000,000	Mrs. Lee Moor of El Paso, Tex.	American Bible Society; Board of Missions to Jews
1,039,000	Mrs. R. W. Kelley of New York	Yale University; Johns Hopkins Hospital; New York Hospital
2,700,000	T. Munroe Dobbins of Philadelphia	30 charitable institutions
4,000,000	Claud H. Foster of Cleveland	15 hospitals and orphanages; Western Reserve University
30,000,000	George R. White of Boston	Hospitals and other philanthropies
1,000,000	Newcomb Cleveland of Scarsdale, N.Y.	Mt. Holyoke College
1,000,000	Dr. H. L. Kretschmer of Chicago	Northwestern University
1,000,000	Abram K. Wright of Clearfield, Pa.	Princeton University
1,500,000	Miss Marie Spear of Scarsdale, N.Y.	Federation of Protestant Welfare
10,000,000	John D. Rockefeller, Jr.	Metropolitan Museum of Art
1,000,000	Mrs. Louis Blaustein of Baltimore	Jewish Medical Center
1,000,000	Mrs. John Hoober of York, Pa.	Religious and educational institutions
2,500,000	A. T. Ashton of Philadelphia, Pa.	University of Pennsylvania
2,000,000	William P. Phillips of Philadelphia, Pa.	Haverford College
1,350,000	E. E. Worthing of Houston	Scholarship fund for Negroes
87,700,000	Mrs. M. A. Wilks of Greenwich, Conn.	63 institutions
1,500,000	Frank J. Gould of New York	New York University
1,000,000	Anonymous donor	Dartmouth College

1953

Amount	From	To
$ 4,000,000	Mrs. Thomas W. Lamont of New York	Smith College; Barnard College; other institutions
4,000,000	Stuard Hirschman of New York	Henrietta and Stuard Hirschman Foundation
2,500,000	Mrs. A. McA. Upshur of San Marino, Calif.	Several educational and philanthropic institutions
1,000,000	Mrs. Margaret G. Hinkley of Brooklyn, N.Y.	Church Charity Foundation (P.E.) of Long Island
10,000,000	Clyde H. Harris of Pendleton, Ore.	Seventh-Day Adventist Church
11,000,000	Frederick H. Prince of Newport, R.I.	Prince Charitable Trust
5,000,000	Mrs. Lolita Sheldon Armour of Chicago	Income to Illinois Institute of Technology; St. Luke's Hospital; Chicago Community Chest
1,475,000	Mrs. Elizabeth E. W. Adams	Yale University
3,000,000	Samuel D. Riddle of Media, Pa.	Hospital
2,000,000	Walter A. Preston of Omaha, Neb.	Yale University
1,125,000	Dr. Joseph Collins of New York	Joseph Collins Foundation
1,000,000	Mrs. Joseph M. Cudahy of Waukegan, Ill.	Several philanthropic institutions
1,200,000	Ellis L. Phillips of Plandome, L.I.	Cornell University
6,000,000	Rockefeller Family of New York	Grand Teton National Park, Wyoming
2,172,000	Dr. Albert A. Berg of New York	New York University
1,750,000	(same)	New York Public Library
717,000	(same)	6 other educational and religious causes
1,000,000	F. J. Sensenbrenner of Chilton, Wis.	Several hospitals, churches, orphanages, and educational institutions
1,000,000	Anonymous New England Industrialist	Tufts College Medical School
3,000,000	John F. Moors of Boston	Harvard University and Radcliffe College
12,000,000	Mrs. Mary Reynolds Babcock of Winston-Salem, N. C.	A charitable and educational foundation

The Desire to Give Persists

Why is it that the wealthy people of America are giving funds to philanthropy—contrary to predictions—more generously than they did in the days of lower income and estate taxes? Certainly, taxes are absorbing vastly more of their income than ever before. Frederick Lewis Allen points out in his recent book, *The Big Change,* that in 1900 Andrew Carnegie had a personal income of $23,000,000, with no income taxes to pay.

There are four major reasons, from my experience, why the generosity of America's wealthy men and women has confounded the "experts" in recent years. Let us briefly discuss them.

First, a financial reason—the new technique for building a capital estate. Because of the heavy income taxes many men of our generation are not taking all of their annual incomes out of their businesses but are leaving them to accumulate and multiply as capital assets.

For instance, I have a friend who started his business career forty-odd years ago, with a capital of one hundred and fifty dollars. He has made a spectacular success in business and has provided a more than comfortable living for his family, has paid large corporation and private income taxes, and has given annually the full allowable 15 per cent (now 20 per cent) of his net income to various philanthropies. But he has also left a major share of his earnings in his business and has thus built a capital worth of over twenty million dollars—representing his equity in his several business enterprises. Further, he has set up a philanthropic foundation to which much of this capital will in due time be transferred.

How did he acquire this large capital fortune in spite of heavy income taxes? Simply by not taking all net earnings out of his business. Had he taken the net earnings out each year, he would have paid about 75 per cent of them to the government in personal income taxes and would now be worth approximately $4,000,000, not $20,000,000. Instead, he has plowed much of the earnings back into his various enterprises, which have prospered and expanded. In so doing, he has been able to employ more people gainfully, and has built up capital assets of many millions

which will serve the well-being of the nation for generations after
he himself passes on. This is but one illustration of thousands
in which men of our time are able, in spite of pessimistic
prophecies, to accumulate vast fortunes for the ultimate benefit
of philanthropy.

Second, the traditional reason. Giving is an honored American
tradition so deeply rooted in our free way of life that it is not
lightly set aside by the imposition of new taxes or by any other
social phenomenon. The American citizen has found his richest
satisfactions in his support of voluntary civic efforts to create a
better world. I dare prophesy that he always will. He remains
loyal to this magnificent tradition of American democracy.

Third, the spiritual reason. There is so much to be done to
bring about a world of civilized well-being and brotherhood. The
ideals and the work of our philanthropic institutions continue
to inspire and compel the socially minded men and women of
our generation to invest great sums of money for the common
good, even though taxes are huge and onerous.

Fourth, America's expanded economy. The prophecy as to the
dissipation of wealth and the demise of the goose that laid the
golden eggs was based upon the assumption that the national
economy would remain static. Naturally then, if our annual
income had remained at ninety billion dollars—the largest it
ever was prior to the making of these prophecies—and if the
Federal Government were still to impose new taxes, which have
now reached $65,000,000,000, plain arithmetic would verify the
fear that there would be nothing left for philanthropy—or even
to live on.

GIVING IN AN EXPANDING ECONOMY

But our national economy has *not* remained static. The national income has shot up to unanticipated heights—for the past
several years it has stayed around $260,000,000,000 per year, three
times what it was in the lush 1920's. The 1952 rate was estimated
to be $284,000,000,000.

A large proportion of this new income derives from products
and services that were not even dreamed of twenty years ago, or
at best were only in the research stage. Most of the large for-

tunes of a generation ago were based upon our natural resources, such as iron and steel, coal, timber, oil, gold, farm lands, city real estate; upon the construction of railways; or upon the creation of our banking and merchandizing systems.

Today, there has been added a vast array of new products: chemicals, electronics, synthetic textiles, pharmaceuticals, metals, hybrid grains and fruits, plastics, antibiotics, prefabricated buildings, synthetic rubbers and fibers, new breeds of animals and fowls, new fertilizers and grasses; gasoline- or electric-powered machines for home, farm, office, and industry; and thousands of other manufactured items, as well as improved processes for manufacturing and distributing wealth.

America has vaulted into a new national economy; we are now producing wealth beyond the dreams of a short quarter century ago. This startling advance into a new era of production and of wealth is, as Alfred P. Sloan noted, due—in considerable degree—to the philanthropic gifts to education made during the past three centuries by men and women who pioneered the schools and colleges of America before education received tax support. The cumulative effect of their devotion has resulted in the present ability of highly educated America to create the new products and processes which are now the basis of much of our present and future wealth. For this wealth is not dependent so much upon the natural resources with which our nation was so generously endowed as upon the creative brains of men and women who are devising ways of making new products for the use of each new generation.

It was this dynamic, or explosive, character of the free American economy that Stalin and the Kremlin misjudged in their cold-war plans. They are said to have expected a collapse of our "tired capitalism" after World War II—at which time of confusion and frustration Russian communism would move in. But our economy is not tired. It is active and dynamic. Our frontiers are not closed. Older geographic frontiers have been replaced by a hundred new frontiers—of research, of imagination, of the creative genius of free men and women—frontiers that reach up into the air waves, through the soil, down into the depths of the sea, across the length and breadth of the land.

For these four major, and other minor, reasons the prophets of doom for private philanthropy sounded a false alarm. Some will undoubtedly choose to remain at the wailing wall. But the philanthropic leaders who have conviction about the vigor of the voluntary element in Americans, and who understand the dynamic nature of our present economy, will continue to find men and women of large resources who will respond sympathetically and generously to their appeals for support.

CHAPTER XIII

Tax Savings on Philanthropic Gifts by Individuals and Corporations

ALMOST invariably during the past forty years the Treasury Department has viewed taxpayers' bona-fide contributions to philanthropy with sympathy and co-operation, seldom challenging deductions for charitable purposes unless there had been some clear indication of impropriety. Further reference will be made in the chapter on foundations (Chapter XIV) to recent amendments to the tax law which recognize and correct certain obvious improprieties.

There has been only one period when the Federal Government seemed to adopt an attitude of actual hostility toward claims to legal deductions for charitable contributions. That was in 1934, in the early days of the New Deal, when conservative elements of the nation were shocked by the size of the Federal Government's new levies. In the preceding chapter we cited several public utterances of outstanding philanthropic leaders in which they prophesied—erroneously as the event proved—that the burdensome taxation would dry up philanthropic giving.

Certain leaders of the New Deal, angered by this mounting wave of criticism, threatened in retaliation to terminate the 15 per cent provision. At that time one of the officers of the Treasury Department told the author that if this chorus of complaints did not "pipe down," people would find themselves really in trouble, with no further recognition of *any* deductions for charitable gifts. He spoke with animus that suggested a contempt for the slow processes of voluntary philanthropy as against the sudden moves of a well-financed Federal Government determined to bring about social and economic changes instanter, without much concern for the wisdom and experience of erstwhile leaders in the field of social undertakings.

This threat did not materialize in executive action or congressional law. The Treasury Department under the New Deal and the Fair Deal has continued—with the exception of this flare-up in 1934—a sympathetic attitude toward charitable gifts.

INCOME TAX DEDUCTIONS ON CAPITAL GIFTS OF SECURITIES AND PROPERTY

The federal income tax had been made possible by the 16th Amendment to the Constitution, ratified February 3, 1913. In the Income Tax Law written at that time, and in all subsequent laws enacted by Congress, provision was made to permit an income tax payer to make deductions of contributions to organized philanthropy from his income prior to taxes. From 1913 to 1952 these allowable deductions were limited to 15 per cent of gross adjusted net income. In July, 1952, the allowable deduction was increased to 20 per cent.

This provision has been a great encouragement to generous individuals throughout the nation and of real assistance in their plans for making substantial gifts to philanthropic, religious, and educational institutions.

The income tax laws also contain another provision, not generally realized, which is a great encouragement to donors. This section provides that if an income tax payer makes a charitable contribution of securities or property which are more valuable than when he acquired them, he may receive credit on his income tax for their present value as deductible from net income before taxes, and need not pay an income tax on the increase of present value over the purchase price. In order to gain this advantage, the taxpayer must give the security or property intact to the philanthropy. If he should sell it, and then turn the proceeds of the sale over to charity, he would be required to pay a capital gains tax on the increase in value.

INCOME TAX PAYERS CONTRIBUTING 90 PER CENT OF THEIR NET INCOME

There is another interesting provision in the Income Tax Law which encourages large-income recipients to make generous gifts. This section provides that if a taxpayer contributes 90 per cent of his net income to organized philanthropy each year for ten successive years, he need not thereafter restrict his charitable deductions to the legal 15 per cent (now 20 per cent). After such a ten-year period of benevolences, he may deduct from his net income his total contributions to charity, whether they be 20 per cent, 50 per cent, or even 100 per cent.

When the so-called Ruml Amendment to the Income Tax Law was enacted recently, to collect this year's income tax "this" year instead of "next" year, the wording of that particular clause was not properly changed. Consequently, the provision has been in suspense during the past few years. It is believed that this failure to change the wording of the clause was inadvertent. Efforts are now being made to amend the wording so as to re-activate the original provision.

TAX SAVINGS ON PHILANTHROPIC GIFTS BY CORPORATIONS

The Income Tax Law—now allowing individuals a 20 per cent deduction—also permits corporations to deduct 5 per cent of net income before taxation for contributions to organized philanthropy. This subject is discussed at length in Chapter XV.

Following are tables which show the saving in personal in-

RELATIONSHIP OF CONTRIBUTIONS TO FEDERAL INCOME TAXES
UNDER THE 1952 ACT WHICH PERMITS PERSONAL
DEDUCTIONS FOR CONTRIBUTIONS TOTALING 20% OF NET INCOME

Taxable Income for Single Persons	Total 20% Contribution Allowed by Law	Tax Saved If Full 20% Donated	Tax Saved per $ by Making a Contribution
$ 2,000	$ 400	$ 88	$ .22
6,000	1,200	348	.29
10,000	2,000	760	.38
14,000	2,800	1,296	.48
20,000	4,000	2,300	.59
26,000	5,200	3,384	.66
32,000	6,400	4,284	.67
44,000	8,800	6,224	.72
50,000	10,000	7,380	.75
60,000	12,000	9,200	.77
70,000	14,000	11,080	.80
80,000	16,000	13,100	.83
90,000	18,000	15,140	.85
100,000	20,000	17,300	.88
150,000	30,000	27,000	.90
200,000	40,000	36,400	.91

come taxes and in corporation taxes which allowable deductions make possible—*provided* the full 20 per cent deductions are claimed by individuals and the full 5 per cent by corporations.

In the consideration of these tax deductions, it should be remembered that men do not give to philanthropy primarily to reduce federal taxes. On the contrary, they give to philanthropy because they want to help constructive causes in which they believe. Tax deductions are a secondary factor that encourages giving, and frequently makes it feasible to increase the amount and effectiveness of a gift.

Corporations with income subject to excess profits taxes can make substantial contributions in their own name to a charitable organization at a net cost of only 19 per cent. The remaining 81 per cent is, in effect, contributed by the United States Treasury through the tax saved by the corporation.

Amount of Gift	Net Cost to Corporation	Balance Paid Through Tax Saving
$ 5,555	$ 1,000	$ 4,555
27,780	5,000	22,780
55,550	10,000	45,555
138,890	25,000	113,890

The above schedule pertains to those corporations in the excess profits tax brackets.

The amount of the gift, of course, is limited for tax purposes to 5 per cent of the corporation's *net income*.

For a corporation which is not subject to excess profits tax a good rule-of-thumb would be that Uncle Sam stands 30% of the contributions and the taxpaying corporation 70%.

PART SIX

What Are the Trends?

CHAPTER XIV

The Philanthropic Foundation—An
American Institution

NO DISCUSSION of philanthropy can be complete without reference to the foundations which have been established for the specific support of philanthropy. They have long been important in the development of American culture, but it was only in the early years of the twentieth century—when John D. Rockefeller and Andrew Carnegie gave the hundreds of millions of dollars to establish the great foundations which bear their names—that this modern institution began to exert its greatest influence.

The term has been in use for many centuries in connection with endowments given to universities, cathedrals, hospitals, and other institutions, where the principal was to remain intact and the annual income to be used for the active work of the institution. In America, such endowments were established from the earliest days. Many set up two or three hundred years ago are still serving the purposes to which they were originally dedicated. Benjamin Franklin, for instance, left bequests to Boston and to Philadelphia with specific stipulations as to how the money was to be invested and reinvested, and for just what charitable purposes the income should be used.

We now use the term *foundation* to describe a type of philanthropic trust fund or endowment that has grown up within the past eighty years. The modern foundation is a fund that has been established independently—not connected with any particular university, hospital, or other institution. It is usually incorporated under the laws of a given state as a nonprofit corporation, and its trustees have the responsibility of distributing the annual income or, in some instances, the principal in accordance with the terms of the incorporation.

The first such independent foundation in America of national significance was the Peabody Education Fund, established in 1867 by a gift of $3,000,000 from George Peabody. The trustees were commissioned to use the fund for "intellectual, moral, and industrial education among the southern and south-western states." In the post-Civil War days it exerted a great influence upon the education of Negroes, and upon the development of the state systems of public education in the South.

Some of the men who served as agents and trustees of the Peabody Education Fund were similarly active in the formative years of the General Education Board which was created by John D. Rockefeller, Sr., in 1902, and in the Rockefeller Foundation, created by the same philanthropist in 1913.

Undoubtedly, the largest family fortune ever devoted to philanthropy is that of three generations of the Rockefeller family. Their gifts to philanthropy are said to have totaled approximately one billion dollars. A major portion of this enormous volume of giving has been to the several foundations set up by the members of the family, including the General Education Board, The Rockefeller Foundation, the Laura Spelman Rockefeller Memorial, the International Educational Board, and the Rockefeller Brothers Fund. Three generations of the family—the world's greatest philanthropists—have put their positive stamp of approval upon the foundation as an effective means for dispensing funds for service to their fellow men.

I shall not attempt a description or an appraisal of the organization and methods of these and other national foundations. There is ample literature on the subject, including a recent volume by Dr. Abraham Flexner entitled *Funds and Foundations*, and one by Raymond Fosdick entitled *The Story of the Rockefeller Foundation*. It is sufficient here to say that the professional staffs, procedures, and appropriations of the Rockefeller and Carnegie Foundations have exerted a profound influence for good upon American and world civilization during the past half century.

One word of discriminating description or definition of objectives may be appropriate. Dr. Frederick Keppel, late president

of the Carnegie Corporation, already quoted, makes this il-
luminating distinction in his book, *The Foundation*:

> The purely charitable trusts, important as they are as evidence of
> the spirit of human brotherhood and in view of the individuals whose
> lives are made happier thereby, are of less significance to the com-
> munity than the foundations—whose purpose is *constructive rather
> than palliative* and which have to do with *educational, scientific and
> social progress.*

In this chapter I shall try only to indicate the scope of present-day philanthropic foundations and the manner in which
they add materially to the amounts of money made available each
year for the support of our philanthropic agencies.

In 1947 the Treasury Department estimated that there were
10,000 philanthropic foundations in America. More recent informal estimates put the present figure at 16,000. The latest
figure comes from Raymond Rich Associates, whose American
Foundations Information Service is engaged in research covering
the entire country in preparation for the seventh edition of
the reference work, *American Foundations and Their Fields.*
This organization estimates that there are approximately 4,000
foundations which qualify under the usual definition of a foundation.

The Ford Foundation—probably the largest of this group—
received from the estate of the late Henry Ford an equity in
the Ford Motor Company which has been variously estimated
to have a value of from a half billion to a billion dollars, compared with the present three hundred and twenty million in the
Rockefeller Foundation. The Ford Foundation has recently
created a staff and an organization that promise to rank it in
importance equal to the older Rockefeller Foundation and the
Carnegie Corporation. The officers of this enormous new foundation have stated that its major aim is *world peace,* and it has
set up and financed several subsidiaries with special aims within
that general compass. The scope of its total program is breath-
taking.

HOW FOUNDATIONS OPERATE

What is the place of foundations in philanthropy's role in American life? As a matter of practical wisdom, many of them have been created for the useful and proper purpose of enabling the donor to give more to philanthropy than he would be able to do without this incorporated trust fund—because of federal income taxation.

This is how such a philanthropic foundation is set up and operates:

A man of wealth finds that he would like to give away each year a large surplus of his income which he does not need for any personal use. He therefore creates a philanthropic foundation under the laws of his state. Let us say he is the chief stockholder in a corporation. He gives the foundation a block of the stock of that corporation. Thereafter, the dividends on that stock are paid to the foundation, and its directors can give away all the income to the philanthropies of their choice, during that year, without any deduction of income tax.

Here is an actual illustration of how it works: a certain man has created a foundation; he was also the creator of a business which has prospered enormously; he has given to his foundation $25,000,000 of the corporation's stock; the stock pays a dividend of approximately one million dollars a year into the treasury of the foundation—whose directors give that million dollars away *in toto*, minus expenses, year by year, to philanthropy.

Had this man *not* established his foundation, he would have received the dividends himself, but he would have had to pay federal income tax on them of about $900,000, leaving him less than $100,000 per year available for philanthropy. Thus, the establishment of his foundation has meant the annual gift of over $900,000 more to philanthropy than would otherwise have been possible.

Many foundations have been established on a much smaller scale—some with capital resources of only a few thousand dollars. But the principle of increasing the annual amount available for philanthropy continues to operate, provided the donor is trying to be of service rather than merely trying to avoid income taxes.

Undoubtedly some persons have made improper use of personal foundations for tax-dodging purposes, but such acts are more and more being closely checked by the government.

In 1950, Congress passed some amendments to the tax laws which ended certain improper practices. Treasury agents had discovered that some people who had established personal foundations proceeded to pay themselves salaries as officers of the foundations. Others arranged for their foundations to loan them their capital funds at low interest, or none at all. Still others made annual appropriations to the foundations out of their 15 per cent allowable deductions from net income for charitable gifts, but then permitted these funds to accumulate in the foundations without making any annual gifts to charity from the foundations. These and other improprieties were corrected by the enactments of 1950.

There are many so-named foundations that are not real foundations, in the sense that they have meager if any funds to distribute. Certain causes which need funds have taken corporate names which include the word "foundation," and have then proceeded to try to raise the funds they need. By terming themselves foundations they give themselves the appearance of a financial stability which does not actually exist—at least at the outset of their activity. Consequently, we occasionally encounter a so-called philanthropic foundation with meager resources which is actually a fund-raising agency. I know of one such "foundation" that exists from day to day only by the grace of the checks that may happen to come in the morning mail.

Following are a few of the larger foundations—named in the order of their founding—with an indication of the sources of the fortunes which endowed them:

Name of Foundation	Year Founded	Founder
The General Education Board	1902	John D. Rockefeller
The Milbank Memorial Fund	1905	Mrs. Elizabeth Milbank Anderson
The Russell Sage Foundation	1907	Mrs. Russell Sage
The Carnegie Corporation	1911	Andrew Carnegie
The Rockefeller Foundation	1913	John D. Rockefeller

Name of Foundation	Year Founded	Founder
Julius Rosenwald Fund	1917	Julius Rosenwald, of Sears-Roebuck
The Commonwealth Fund	1918	Edward S. Harkness
The Juilliard Musical Foundation	1920	Augustus D. Juilliard
The Kresge Foundation	1924	S. S. Kresge
The Duke Endowment	1924	James B. Duke
The Guggenheim Foundation	1925	John S. Guggenheim
The Buhl Foundation	1927	Henry Buhl, of Boggs & Buhl Department Store
The Markle Foundation	1927	John Markle, of Markle Coal Company
The S. H. Kress Foundation	1929	Samuel H. Kress
The Children's Fund of Michigan	1929	James Couzens, of Ford Motor Company
The W. K. Kellogg Foundation	1930	W. K. Kellogg, of Kellogg Cereal Products
The Mellon Educational & Charitable Trust	1930	Andrew W. Mellon, of the Mellon Bank
The Louis D. Beaumont Foundation, Inc.	1933	Louis D. Beaumont
The Alfred P. Sloan Foundation	1934	Alfred P. Sloan, of General Motors
Surdna Foundation	1935	John E. Andrus
The John A. Hartford Foundation	1935	John A. Hartford, of Great Atlantic & Pacific Tea Company
The Ford Foundation	1936	Ford family, of Ford Motor Company
M. D. Anderson Foundation	1936	M. D. Anderson
Charles Hayden Foundation Endowment, Inc.	1937	Charles Hayden, of Hayden, Stone & Co.
The Lilly Foundation	1937	Josiah Kirby Lilly
The Olin Foundation, Inc.	1938	Franklin W. Olin
The Avalon Foundation	1940	Mrs. Ailsa Mellon Bruce
The James Foundation	1941	Arthur Curtiss James
The Old Dominion Fund	1941	Paul Mellon, of Mellon Bank
The Cullen Foundation	1947	Hugh R. Cullen, of Independent Oil Company
The Pew Memorial Foundation	1948	The Pew family, of Sun Oil Company
Benwood Foundation	1950	George Thomas Hunter, of Coca-Cola Corporation
The Fleischmann Foundation	1951	Max C. Fleischmann, of Fleischmann Yeast Co.

Philanthropic foundations have become such an important factor in contemporary American life that their operations have recently become the object of inquiry by a special committee of Congress. Exhaustive questionnaires were sent to the heads of foundations, and several foundation officers were called to Washington to testify before the committee. The original purpose seemed to be to investigate possible subversive influences that might have been financed by foundations, but the inquiry brought out a much wider range of information. It seemed, in my opinion, to instruct and to reassure the American people as to the usefulness of these philanthropic agencies. Certainly some errors have been made in appropriations by foundations but, on balance, their records of giving appear excellent.

Dr. Abraham Flexner, for many years a wise counselor of the Carnegie Foundation and of the General Education Board, says in his recent book, *Funds and Foundations*:

Wise or unwise use may be made of funds thus contributed, but the wisdom or unwisdom is in the main the wisdom or unwisdom of the persons who, or institutions which, spend the money, rarely—perhaps I might say *never*—of the original donor. . . .

In the total view, then, especially as regards the pioneering educational and scientific achievements of philanthropy, the endowed foundation stands out, beyond question, as one of the great bulwarks of the American Way.

CHAPTER XV

A Growing Trend in Corporation Support

PHILANTHROPY in America is an enormous enterprise. Taken as a whole, it now receives voluntary gifts of approximately $4,250,000,000 a year. This is in addition to many billions of dollars which it receives from other sources, such as student tuitions and fees in colleges, fees from patients in hospitals, membership and service fees received by such organizations as the Boy Scouts, and so on.

But in spite of this four-and-a-quarter-billion-dollar voluntary giving, our community agencies could use to excellent advantage, and for the good of the nation, much additional income. *There are still two great undeveloped reservoirs of potential support.*

The first is in the pockets and bank accounts of *individuals* who are not using nearly the full 20 per cent of their net income which the Treasury Department now allows as deductions on federal income taxes. On current income tax returns the American people are reporting about 2½ to 3 per cent of net income in charitable gifts. If all were to make gifts up to the permissible 20 per cent, our voluntary agencies would have something like twenty-seven billion dollars more a year to spend. It is my belief that they could spend this sum more wisely and with greater benefit to our people than it could be spent in any other way. This would vastly aid the country to raise its standards and goals in the only field where there is conspicuous underproduction—the field of spiritual and cultural values, those values on the top planes of our civilization.

The constant increase in personal giving has been because philanthropic agencies *have* succeeded in persuading larger and larger numbers of men and women that money thus given will do good and bring satisfaction. This continuous *education of the public* is a primary and perennial task. Hence, development programs, publicity, public relations, fund raising.

150

UNDEVELOPED RESOURCES

The other reservoir of unrealized income lies in the treasuries of *corporations*. The Treasury Department permits a corporation to give 5 per cent of its net income, before taxes, to philanthropy. This annual net income amounts roughly to about twenty-five billion dollars. If corporations were to give 5 per cent of this net, it would provide a billion and a quarter dollars a year for charitable purposes.

As a matter of fact, corporations are now giving at the rate of one fifth of that amount, or about $250,000,000 a year.

This two-hundred-fifty-million-dollar level represents a decided increase in corporation giving during the past dozen years. There is ample evidence of a definite trend, throughout the nation, toward steadily increasing support by corporations of both local and national philanthropic projects.

In 1938, the United States Treasury Department reported that approximately twenty-seven million dollars appeared on the tax returns of corporations as gifts to privately financed agencies. Thus, present corporation giving is approximately ten times that of 1938. There is evidence on every hand.

Last year over 750 corporations made gifts to a certain national religious agency with an interdenominational program of service.

One utility corporation announced a gift of $175,000 to the Community Fund of its city.

Within the past two years one industrial corporation announced a grant of a million dollars to an institution of higher education—probably the largest single gift to education ever made by a business concern.

Recent studies of public opinion show that a substantial majority of stockholders approve corporation gifts to philanthropy.

It is interesting to note the per cent of net profit which the different industrial groups contribute to philanthropic causes, according to Andrews: mining and quarrying 0.30; manufacturing 0.66; public utilities 0.46; trade 1.15; service 1.29; finance, insurance, real estate, lessors of real property 0.43; construction 0.84; agriculture, forestry, and fishery 0.47.

The Treasury Department does not break down its statistics to reveal what categories of private philanthropic agencies receive the most corporation support. At present the only way in which such information can be obtained is by the sampling method. Recently the National Industrial Conference Board made known the results of such a study, covering the giving record of "79 of the 100 largest manufacturing corporations in the United States," and reported the following findings:

> *Community Chests* receive the largest total of gifts from these 79 corporations: the median gift in this category was $44,858. The *Red Cross* and the *hospitals* received substantial support, and gifts to *colleges and universities* increased over corresponding gifts by the same corporations in 1948.
>
> Gifts to these institutions, which at one time represented an exception to corporation giving, are now generally made in accordance with the direct benefit theory. These contributions are to be distinguished from corporate funds to colleges for the purpose of research. The latter are generally charged as a business expense rather than a charitable donation.
>
> Gifts to colleges and universities range from $100 to $235,000—with the median coming to $7,600.

State laws vary considerably in their attitude toward corporation giving to private philanthropy, but in many states there is no legal restriction against it when exercised for the public good.

In other states where there is a legislative brake on corporation giving, the interpretation of the courts has been increasingly liberal, if the intent has been shown to be constructive.

The Commission on Financing Higher Education—established under sponsorship of the Association of American Universities —published a report in 1952, entitled *Higher Education and American Business*, which gives interesting information on the legal aspects of corporation giving. It cites twenty-three states which have "adopted statutes expressly authorizing, in one form or another, corporate contributions for philanthropic purposes." Mr. F. Emerson Andrews adds four more in his book *Corporation Giving*. These twenty-seven states are:

Arkansas	Maine	North Carolina
California	Maryland	Ohio
Colorado	Massachusetts	Oklahoma
Connecticut	Michigan	Pennsylvania
Delaware	Minnesota	Tennessee
Hawaii	Missouri	Texas
Illinois	New Jersey	Virginia
Indiana	New Mexico	West Virginia
Kansas	New York	Wisconsin

The Commission also presents an encouraging summary of interpretations by the courts in their application of the common law to corporation philanthropy.

Thoughtful people, including many corporation heads, believe that the business concerns of America—which now account for one half of our national wealth and 40 per cent of our annual income—should in their own corporate self-interest take a greater share in the maintenance of privately supported agencies. The present trend of increasing support certainly reflects such a growing sense of responsibility. Management is reflecting a greater interest in the nongovernmental civic endeavors which minister to the general well-being of the American people. There seem to be at least four major reasons for this trend:

1. For the highest success corporations require employees of sound character, high intelligence, and vigorous health. It is the primary function of America's private philanthropic agencies to foster these very attributes.

2. Corporations also require a consumer public of similar high standards. Consumer studies have shown time and again that industry does not sell its products to illiterate, shiftless, or unhealthy sections of the public. Corporations have a direct self-interest in the general intelligence and morality of American society.

3. The newly discovered wealth of America will not be dug out of the ground, but will be created by ideas of educated and resourceful men and women. Future frontiers of America are no longer physical frontiers; they are frontiers of knowledge and of the bold application of such knowledge. There are prosperous industries today—employing

scores of thousands of people and creating hundreds of millions of new wealth—that did not exist ten years ago.

4. Corporation prosperity depends in no small measure upon the inherent vigor of free enterprise. Today the most perfect demonstration of American free enterprise is that vast network of beneficent agencies supported by the voluntary gifts of men and women who are concerned about the spiritual and moral fiber of the American people.

There are three manifestations of free society in America that seem to me so closely interwoven that no one of them can be weakened, lest our whole free structure disintegrate: they are local self-government, voluntary giving, and free enterprise in business.

Corporations can give heavily burdened directors of private agencies a much-needed boost. Is it not to the direct interest of corporations to give their full 5 per cent to these institutions —and thus help to keep them vigorous and enthusiastic demonstrations of free enterprise? If free enterprise is abandoned in American private philanthropy, can it be saved for American business?

Managers and stockholders seem to have a growing conviction that it is desirable, for the four reasons given above, for corporations to make generous contributions to the instrumentalities that mean so much to the moral and economic fiber of our Republic.

FURTHER DEVELOPMENT OF CORPORATION GIVING NEEDS PATIENT CULTIVATION

It should not be supposed that corporations are suddenly going to increase their philanthropic giving up to the legally allowable maximum. But the trend is clearly upward, and many leaders are urging their fellow officers, directors, and stockholders in this direction.

Vigorous appeals to this effect have been recently made by the heads of America's two largest corporations: Frank W. Abrams, chairman of the board of the Standard Oil Company of New Jersey, and Alfred P. Sloan, Jr., chairman of the board of General Motors. These impressive public statements have been supplemented by other industrial leaders, such as Henry Ford, II, and Laird Bell, of Chicago. The National Association of Manufacturers issued an official communication, at a recent annual convention, urging that member corporations vigorously support our educational and philanthropic institutions.

Mr. Sloan, widely known for his gifts to cancer research represented in the Sloan-Kettering Institute, has repeatedly proposed that private enterprise give special aid to higher education. The Sloan Foundation, which he set up, has contributed generously to a number of colleges and universities.

In his article "Big Business Must Help Our Colleges," which appeared in *Collier's* for June 2, 1951, Mr. Sloan makes a strong case: "it is vital—if we are to perpetuate our free society—that we find a way to keep our colleges, universities and technological institutions virile, progressive and, above all else, free. To stay that way they must have adequate financial support." He then points out industry's continuing debt to education. He says that industry must insure an expanding reservoir of what he calls "fundamental knowledge"—the discovery of which "starts in the academic area as pure research." He believes firmly that "the logical place to develop this fundamental knowledge on a broad scale is at our educational and technical institutions," which "operate in a climate conducive to fundamental thinking"; and that "in our own interest, corporate enterprise should support the sources from which fundamental knowledge flows," both in the natural and in the social sciences, or humanities.

He concludes:

Our corporations spend many millions to provide medical and welfare benefits for their employees. They have just as much responsibility, I believe, to contribute to the common cause of higher education. In the long view, these donations would contribute to the advance of our living standards, and to the strengthening of our national security, and that affects the lives of all Americans.

This present-day attitude on the part of prominent corporation executives is in sharp contrast to attitudes in evidence only a half dozen years ago. I well recall the blazing anger shown by the man second in charge of one of the world's greatest financial

institutions, during an interview in 1946, when it was suggested
that his corporation make a grant to the college of which he was
an alumnus and a trustee. Said he, with rising vocal vehemence:
"Give me one ——— ——— good reason why any ——— corporation should make a gift to any ——— college! You can't
convince me!"

And a year later the head of a world-famous manufacturing
concern said, when asked to recommend that his corporation
make a grant to a great scientific and engineering institution:
"Not on your life. Our business is to make dividends for our
stockholders—not gifts for education!"

But the climate has greatly changed in the past three years,
under the leadership of such industrialists as those named above.

Granted this unmistakable trend, it would still be just as
naïve to expect all our corporations immediately to increase
their giving to the full 5 per cent as it would be to expect our
forty million individual taxpayers immediately to increase theirs
up to their full allowable maximum. Educational and philanthropic leaders will need to carry on a steady and enlightening
program of cultivation in order to secure from both these great
reservoirs the full measure of potential support.

COMPANY FOUNDATIONS—A NEW TREND

Even the executive who wants to have his corporation make
substantial gifts to philanthropic causes encounters difficulties
within his own management, unless of course his is a closely
owned business.

If the president, for instance, is a trustee of a given college
and asks for a corporation grant of $25,000 to his Alma Mater,
the vice-president may counter with a request for a like grant
to his favorite hospital. The result has frequently been a stand-
off, with neither gift approved. There are other difficulties, such
as the advice of the corporation counsel to submit each proposed
gift to a vote of the stockholders.

For such reasons many officials are turning to the use of a
company foundation. This plan envisages the stockholders' prior
approval to set aside each year an agreed percentage of net
profits for philanthropic purposes, and authorization for certain

officers to distribute these gifts as their best judgment dictates.
A company foundation is then set up as a nonprofit corporation, with certain officers of the parent corporation as trustees.
The corporation then pays each year to its own foundation the
percentage of net profits which the stockholders have authorized,
and the trustees then distribute this money to philanthropic
agencies whose requests, after proper presentation and examina-
tion, they approve.

One of the first corporations to make use of this method was
the Lehigh Structural Steel Company, of New York and Allen-
town, Pennsylvania, of which Thomas R. Mullen is president.
Mr. Mullen is so enthusiastic about the operation of his company's foundation that he issued a brochure about it which he
has distributed widely. In this pamphlet he discusses the organization of the foundation, its method of operation, and the
effective way in which it is able to co-operate in projects of
especial benefit to its own community—in one recent year it
helped three local hospitals, the Community Chest, and several
welfare and charitable projects.

Recent developments in this relatively new field were well
summarized by F. Emerson Andrews, director of philanthropic
research of Russell Sage Foundation, in the May, 1952, issue of
American Foundations News Service, of New York City:

A wave of foundations of a new type has sprung up in the past
several years. These are corporation foundations, "company" foundations, trusts, funds—under any title, tax-exempt, nonprofit legal entities
separate from the parent company but with trustee boards consisting
wholly or principally of corporation officers and directors, and their
purpose the facilitating of company giving.

How numerous they are is not definitely known, and any estimate
of a few months ago is outmoded today. Russell Sage Foundation's
survey of corporation giving will reveal that although corporation
foundations are still relatively rare, in a random sampling a full 4 per
cent of corporations in the asset group of $1 million or more have
established their own foundations. If this average prevails among the
37,000 corporations in this asset class, there may be as many as 1,500
business-related foundations in the United States today.

Interest on the part of business in forming such foundations reached new heights early this year. Contributing factors may have been a special Kiplinger Letter on "tax-exempt foundations" issued late in December; the emphasis on corporation foundations in the revised booklet, *The Five Per Cent,* of the National Planning Association; special bulletins on this subject by several business advisory services, and— of course—the current high level of corporate taxation, including an excess profits tax.

All organizations able to help in this field felt the new pressures. The Carnegie Foundation for the Advancement of Teaching had more than 300 requests for its *Charters of Philanthropies* in the early part of the year. Publishers of this *News Service* report greatly increased requests for information and specific help from business firms. In the single month of January we received at Russell Sage Foundation 162 inquiries from corporation executives, or legal firms representing them, concerning methods of setting up such foundations.

Some of these inquirers seemed to be seeking a magical incantation against business taxes, but others were carefully studying the advantages of a corporation foundation in bringing order into the present chaos of business giving.

STATE-WIDE COLLEGE FUNDS

Another method now being used to persuade corporations to give more freely to colleges is that of the *college association within a state.* This is a nonprofit incorporation of the independently (nontax-) supported colleges of a state for the purpose of receiving gifts, chiefly from corporations. These gifts are then distributed by the state college association to the member colleges for operating expenses, in accordance with an agreed-upon formula.

The chief purpose of this new device is to eliminate the competitive appeals of the several colleges. Under this plan a corporation receives only one appeal for current support from all the independent colleges of its state. In Indiana, where the plan was early put into operation, corporations have been giving about $150,000 a year to the state's dozen colleges. In Ohio, the plan is producing about $200,000 a year for its twenty member colleges. Twenty-five states and two regions have already created similar state college funds, and 350 colleges are, through them, proceeding hopefully to raise substantial annual support from corporations.

Recently a group of business men incorporated a new organization to stimulate corporate giving to colleges, known as the Council for Financial Aid to Education. The organizers of this Council include five top corporation executives, Frank W. Abrams of Standard Oil of New Jersey, Alfred P. Sloan, Jr., of General Motors, Irving Olds of U. S. Steel, Walter Paepcke of the Container Corporation, and Henning W. Prentis, Jr., of the Armstrong Cork Company.

The Certificate of Incorporation specifies that:

. . . the corporation is not itself to distribute funds to educational institutions or to solicit contributions for such purpose.

This Council proposes:

. . . To serve in an advisory and cooperative capacity, both to prospective contributors and to educational institutions in connection with the formulation, adoption and carrying out of the programs of various kinds having for their general purpose the obtaining of financial support . . .

The same developments which have led the colleges to this concentrated campaign are causing business to take serious thought. Some corporations, which are trying to develop well-ordered policies and programs of their own, are concerned lest this new pressure will throw their own policies off balance. Others, which have as yet developed no active interest in the programs of philanthropy, are apprehensive for less constructive reasons.

Many corporations are now giving top-level attention to their social responsibility for supporting the nation's voluntary agencies—often appointing certain officers to give their entire attention to appeals for contributions, and appointing committees to formulate giving policies and programs. Among the hurdles sometimes encountered are legal liabilities in the form of suits by disgruntled stockholders.

Long-range precautions are being taken by certain corporations against such suits, and court decisions are currently being

sought which will give the green light to philanthropic contributions. An instance is a suit in the Superior Court of New Jersey
which was brought by a group of stockholders of the A. P. Smith
Manufacturing Co., of East Orange, N. J., in protest against the
corporation's gift of $1,500 to Princeton University. This was the
case in brief:

> After announcement of the gift, made to the University's annual
> fund, several of the company's 75 stockholders objected, saying it was
> made for a purpose foreign to the objects of the firm and amounted
> to a misappropriation of company funds.
>
> Represented by Josiah Stryker, they contend the firm's certificate of
> incorporation is a contract between the company and its stockholders.
> They hold also that the gift is banned by federal and state constitu-
> tional provisions barring impairment of contracts and requiring due
> process and just compensation in the taking of personal property.
>
> The company, represented by Waldron M. Ward, then brought suit
> asking the court to define its rights. It cites a 1950 law permitting
> corporations "to discharge their obligations to society" and thus brings
> about the first court test of that law. . . .

Dr. Harold W. Dodds and George A. Brakeley, president and
treasurer respectively of Princeton, testified as to the necessity for
new and additional forms of private giving to our independent
colleges, and Frank W. Abrams, chairman of the board of Standard Oil of New Jersey, argued:

> . . . that corporations pay the colleges nothing for training personnel
> they eagerly recruit each June. American business, he said, neither
> needs nor wants a free ride, least of all from our educational institutions
> which we know to be hard pressed financially.
>
> Under the present tax structure, he said, it is easier for a firm than
> an individual to make such donations. . . . Stockholders and executives
> generally feel it is not good business for corporations to take benefits
> while avoiding normally accepted obligations. . . .

In May, 1953, the Supreme Court of New Jersey ruled that
the contribution was legally valid. Judge Alfred A. Stein in his
ruling said:

Such giving may be called an incidental power, but when it is considered in its essential character, it may well be regarded as a major, though unwritten, corporate power. It is even more than that. In the Court's view of the case it amounts to solemn duty. . . .

This ruling was appealed to the Supreme Court of New Jersey and on June 25, 1953, the high court affirmed Judge Stern's ruling.

It may be assumed that this court case was planned by corporations and educational leaders as a deliberate test of the legal rights of a corporation to make gifts to independent colleges. If this assumption is correct, it is a hopeful sign of the growing sense of responsibility on the part of corporate management for the continued vigor of our nontax-supported institutions.

CHAPTER XVI

The Increasing Volume of
Voluntary Philanthropy

THE enormous increase in social services now performed or aided by the Federal Government has misled many citizens to conclude that private philanthropy in the United States is on the way out. Nothing could be farther from the truth. For in almost every direction it is carrying larger responsibilities than ever. Leaders in the field can see no signs of a letup in the calls upon its generosity, nor in the upward curve that represents its total service to our people.

Actually, this should surprise no one who stops to consider all the kinds of growth still going on in our country. Population mounts steadily. People are living longer. There is constant striving for higher standards in health, education, emotional adjustment, security, and general well-being. Millions of people cannot even measurably reach these goals by their own efforts alone. Many need all the help they can get from every kind of agency, *public and private*.

Doubtless the best way to make this picture clear is to look into the recent statistics of a few typical institutions and services. All figures used are from reliable and authoritative sources. The total evidence leaves no doubt that voluntarily supported services, far from diminishing, are on a steady increase.

HOSPITALS

Let us look first at comparative figures for independent hospitals. In 1934 there was a total of 6,334 hospitals in the United States, with a bed capacity of 1,048,101. In 1950 there were 6,430 hospitals, with a bed capacity of 1,456,912. Of the total number of hospitals in 1934, 2,646 were under *voluntary* philanthropic control, with a total of 267,712 beds. In 1950 the *vol-*

untary hospitals had increased to 3,169, with a capacity of 368,-866 beds. These figures are from the Hospital Number of the *Journal* of the American Medical Association of May, 1951.

The total admissions in these voluntary hospitals have increased at a far greater rate. In 1934, they admitted 4,163,735 patients, whereas in 1950 they admitted 11,253,902.

COLLEGES

Similar growth is indicated by the comparative figures on our independent colleges for 1934 and for 1948. These figures, taken from the statistics issued by the U.S. Office of Education, also show the division between publicly controlled and privately controlled institutions.

In 1934, 1,418 institutions of higher education reported to the United States Office of Education. In 1950—the latest year for which the Office has published its statistics on higher education —a total of 1,868 institutions reported. Of this number, the division between publicly controlled and privately controlled institutions follows, with the enrollment in each group:

INSTITUTIONS OF HIGHER EDUCATION IN THE UNITED STATES

Publicly Controlled

Year	Number	No. of Students
1934	501	529,931
1950	665	1,355,000

Privately Controlled

1934	917	525,429
1950	1,203	1,314,000

In this fourteen-year period there has been an obviously striking increase in the number and capacity of institutions of both types, or we should not have been able to take care of an enrollment two and a half times as great as that of 1934. And there is no prospect of any lessening in the demand for college education.

INDEPENDENT PRIMARY AND SECONDARY SCHOOLS

Though there has lately been much discussion of the relationship between public and private schools—focusing renewed attention on the latter—many people probably still think of private schools as occupying a small and diminishing place. In comparison with the immense enrollments in public schools, their numbers may look small. But they are by no means diminishing—they are steadily growing.

To make the situation concrete, compare a prediction of 1939 with what has happened since. In that year an administrator of the Harvard Graduate School of Education, informally addressing the faculty of one of the largest and strongest preparatory schools for boys, made in essence the following pronouncement:

The private preparatory school in America has its back to the wall. I do not say that you will be closed up in five years, or in ten. But I do say that unless you can prove that you are giving the public and your patrons something superior, something they cannot get elsewhere, your days are numbered.

If meant to imply that the independent preparatory school was on the way out, this prediction has been proved woefully wrong. One wonders at the viewpoint behind it. For the enrollment in both primary and secondary private schools stands at an all-time high. In brief, the situation is as follows—the figures being taken from an article appearing in *School Life*, May, 1950, issued by the Office of Education, Federal Security Agency. The author of the article is Rose Marie Smith, educational statistician, Research and Statistical Service. The figures were culled from her article by the National Council of Independent Schools:

ENROLLMENTS IN NON-PUBLIC SCHOOLS

Year	Elementary	Secondary
1930	2,309,886	373,159
1932	2,384,181	427,978
1934	2,382,251	380,880
1936	2,274,584	415,435
1938	2,263,703	477,951
1940	2,172,273	487,672
1942	2,150,896	512,721
1944	2,187,000	540,000
1946	2,278,390	572,605
1948	2,468,390	629,231
1950	2,754,000	655,000

Miss Smith goes on with these tables, giving estimates for every two years to 1960, when it is anticipated there will be 3,973,000 enrolled in nonpublic elementary schools (kindergarten through Grade 8), and 1,085,000 in secondary schools (Grades 9 through 12).

SOCIAL AND HEALTH SERVICES

In the field of social services, records are equally impressive. In 1932, for instance, contributors responded to the Christmas appeal of *The New York Times* for the "100 Neediest Cases" with $265,000. In 1952, they contributed $385,000.

The *American Red Cross* makes an annual report on the total gifts for both national and chapter objectives. In 1941, the total reported was $23,400,000. In 1951, a comparable peacetime year, it was $77,640,331. There are at present 3,735 chapters.

The *National Foundation for Infantile Paralysis* is one of the largest voluntary health agencies in the nation. In 1933, it started a spectacular series of fund-raising campaigns by celebrating the birthday of President Franklin D. Roosevelt with a series of "President's Balls" throughout the United States, and since that time—with the aid of the March of Dimes—has annually raised large sums for the fight on infantile paralysis. In 1939 the national office of this foundation reported voluntary contributions of $1,600,000; in 1953, of $51,500,000.

The *Heart Association*—a relatively minor organization before its incorporation in 1946—has so stimulated popular interest in combating heart trouble, and has met with such response, that its income and program have expanded by leaps and bounds in the last half dozen years.

The *National Tuberculosis Association*—another important voluntary organization—has for many years raised funds annually by its sale of Christmas Seals. In spite of the increasing responsibility which cities and states have assumed for tuberculosis hospitals and for other phases of the fight on the "white plague," voluntary contributions to the National Tuberculosis Association and its thousands of state and local chapters have steadily risen. In 1932 the contributing public bought seals to the extent of $3,470,000; in 1951 the total rose to $21,717,000.

Community Chests

The free-will contributions to Community Chests have also increased steadily in spite of the belief of many citizens that local social services previously rendered by the member agencies have now been taken over *in toto* by government. Of course, this is not so; well-informed citizens not only have continued their gifts to these co-operative agencies but have increased them. It is difficult to compare the contributions of 1934 with the present, because there are a great many more Community Chests now than there were then—but this very fact is itself evidence that private philanthropy is gaining wider support.

In 1934, voluntary contributors gave $70,000,000 to 399 Chests, according to a report of Community Chests and Councils of America, Inc. In 1952, the Chests had risen to 1,319 and the total gifts to $257,000,000.

The Upsurge of Voluntary Giving

In trying to estimate today's most important trends in the field of practical philanthropy, we have called special attention to three:

1. The increasing calls being made upon it.
2. The distinctively American "foundation," set up in the past chiefly by individuals or families of means, for the very purpose of giving wisely and effectively.
3. The growth in giving by industrial corporations, increasingly through nonprofit foundations organized for the purpose.

All this looks like progress in the field of giving—and it is. As demands have increased, better ways have been found to meet them. Not only has there been improvement in the science and art of fund raising, but there has been businesslike improvement in the administration of benevolent funds and in their effective application to vastly diversified needs.

As a result of all these factors, the *voluntary giving of the American people to philanthropic agencies has risen to unprecedented heights in the past ten years*. There are two reasons for this other than the basic one of increased population and wealth.

We have already discussed these two particular reasons—the creation of the modern campaign method, and the rise of the new profession of fund raising.

If the reader wishes to study the statistical analysis of American philanthropy in general, he would do well to turn to an authoritative publication on this subject by F. Emerson Andrews

CONTRIBUTIONS TO PHILANTHROPY

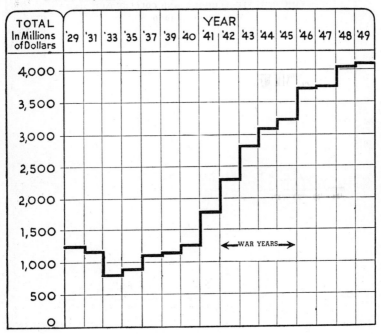

CHART No. 1

of Russell Sage Foundation. This book, entitled *Philanthropic Giving*, is published by the Foundation. In his study Mr. Andrews presents extensive figures on the total volume of philanthropy, its distribution, and its sources.

In this chapter I wish to present three charts illustrating the recent upsurge of giving.

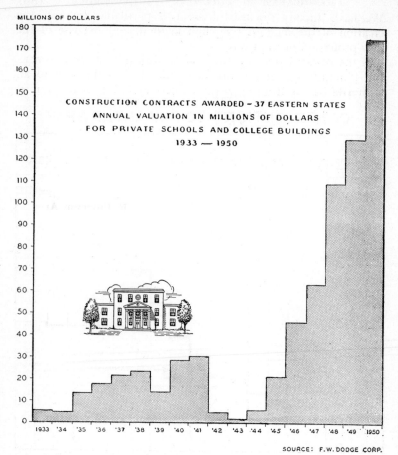

MILLIONS OF DOLLARS

CONSTRUCTION CONTRACTS AWARDED – 37 EASTERN STATES
ANNUAL VALUATION IN MILLIONS OF DOLLARS
FOR PRIVATE SCHOOLS AND COLLEGE BUILDINGS
1933 — 1950

SOURCE: F.W. DODGE CORP.

CHART NO. 2

The first (Chart No. 1) is an approximation of the annual amounts which the American people have given to all philanthropic causes from 1929 to 1950. These figures have been assembled from the reports of Protestant and Catholic churches, the Council of Community Chests, the biennial reports of the United States Office of Education, and other miscellaneous sources.

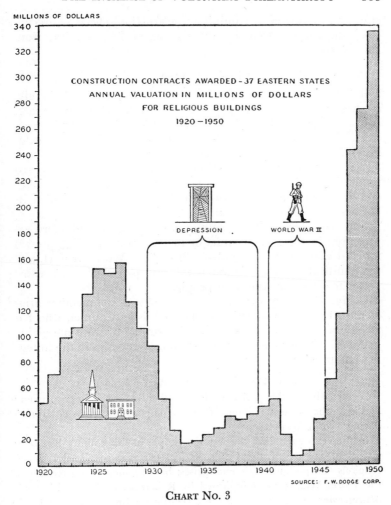

MILLIONS OF DOLLARS

CONSTRUCTION CONTRACTS AWARDED - 37 EASTERN STATES
ANNUAL VALUATION IN MILLIONS OF DOLLARS
FOR RELIGIOUS BUILDINGS
1920 −1950

DEPRESSION

WORLD WAR II

SOURCE: F. W. DODGE CORP.

CHART NO. 3

The second and third charts are taken from figures prepared
by the F. W. Dodge Corporation, which show the twenty-year
record of building construction contracts let by private schools
and colleges (Chart No. 2), and by church organizations (Chart
No. 3). Since these institutions draw most of their income from

gifts, this volume of new building construction reflects indirectly, but with relative accuracy, the volume of their receipts from philanthropy.

UPSURGE OF GIVING IN TIME OF WAR

It may surprise those who have not made a study of the giving habits of the American people to learn that they have greatly *increased* their support of all our voluntary philanthropic agencies *during periods of active war*. In 1942, immediately after Pearl Harbor, many inexperienced boards of trustees of colleges and other civilian institutions called off their proposed fund-raising campaigns for the period of the emergency. Indeed, one of the nation's best-known fund-raising firms suspended its business for the duration of the war.

But other boards of trustees—more optimistic and more experienced in the giving habits of the American public—pressed forward with fund-raising plans throughout World War II, and their institutions came through the war period with increased power to serve the American people.

George E. Lundy—vice-president of one of the member firms of the American Association of Fund-Raising Counsel, who has made one of the most comprehensive studies of war-time giving in America—has given me permission to quote him in the following paragraphs:

WHAT HAPPENED DURING WORLD WAR I?

Fortunately, for this period we have authentic records in government files as to the amount of money that people gave to various enterprises during World War I.

In the years preceding the war the people of this country had been giving an average of about $500,000,000 per year to all educational, religious and philanthropic enterprises; but the sums they gave during the World War years as indicated by Robert R. Doane, in his book, *Measurement of American Wealth* (Harper & Brothers), were far in excess of this amount, as the following comparison reveals:

THREE PREWAR YEARS	
1914-1916 Total given	$1,966,000,000
Yearly average	655,333,000

THREE WAR YEARS

1917-1919 Total given	$3,138,000,000
Yearly average	1,046,000,000

WHAT HAPPENED DURING WORLD WAR II?

As was to be expected, the giving record of our people during the Second World War was almost unbelievable. Note the comparison between the giving and the average annual giving of the people during the four years preceding the war and the four years during the war—as is revealed by figures from Andrews' book, *Philanthropic Giving*, in the following summary.

This great outpouring of gifts attracted wide attention, not only among the leaders of institutions that were concerned, but by businessmen and financial interests as well.

FOUR PREWAR YEARS

1938-1941 Total given	$4,439,000,000
Yearly average	$1,109,000,000

FOUR WAR YEARS

1942-1945 Total given	$10,040,000,000
Yearly average	$2,510,000,000

Mr. Lundy further points out what he has found to be some significant factors in this phenomenon:

There are several reasons why the American people have always given more to philanthropy in wartime. First should be mentioned a basic spiritual and patriotic reason.

Americans love peace, and long and pray and work for World Peace. It is one of the most fundamental purposes in the world. Consequently, when war strikes, we are profoundly shocked, and find it extremely difficult to believe that it has indeed come upon us.

Invariably, this yearning for peace exposes us to unpreparedness; and the shock of finding ourselves in actual danger stirs us, in time, to our maximum efforts. Only thus do we find the strength—the belated strength—to survive.

Another reason for increased philanthropy in wartime lies in the great increase of money in circulation and the simultaneous decrease in the usual opportunities for spending it. With more cash in their hands, people can travel less, buy fewer television sets, refrigerators, clothes and houses.

So we see wartime producing two surpluses—a spiritual surplus of patriotism and public concern, and a financial surplus of ready cash.

This is not to imply that *all* people in America react in this constructive manner to these two wartime surpluses; indeed, many of them do not—as we well know. Some react selfishly. But, as a rule, these latter are not the men and women who build colleges and churches even in peacetime. There are enough fine-grained, patriotic men and women in America who do react unselfishly so that a definite trend of increased generosity in wartime has been established as an historical fact.

PART SEVEN

What of the Future?

CHAPTER XVII

There Are Still Fields to Conquer

MANY new adventures in human betterment beckon voluntary pioneers. May it not be said that, with a generation more generally educated than any previous generation, the opportunities for the extension of peaceful, prosperous, and dignified human society are more exciting than ever?

Who, for instance, can find the key to a world of peace, in which men of all lands may enjoy the products of their minds and bodies without being compelled in each generation to throw them into the cauldron of war?

Who will take the lead in distributing the ample food resources of the world to the hungry billions who have not enough to eat?

Who will solve the appalling problem of the rise in juvenile delinquency and youthful crime?

Who will pioneer in community welfare and health in the mushrooming cities into which a larger and larger proportion of our people is being drawn?

Who will devise the new techniques for developing a free mass market, throughout the world, for the enjoyable products of industry—as they are now shipped across state lines in our United States?

Will these, and other, barriers to human happiness be laid low by *governments* and *laws* and by *tax appropriations*? Certainly *not by them alone*. Not without the lead and stimulus of private citizens who will pioneer on their own initiative, with their own philanthropic funds, driven on by their own vision of a better world.

A delightful commentary on both personal initiative and community interest is found in William Allen White's autobiography. He writes: "Every country editor's job is to conduct, directly or indirectly, his town's drive for progress and benevolence; and it was no new experience for me to pound the streets of Emporia with a subscription paper in my hand. I had done it for twenty years."

FOOD FOR THE HUNGRY MILLIONS

The question of food for the hungry millions of people on the face of the earth is a problem which may seem remote to us. But there are areas in the world where hundreds of thousands of persons die annually from chronic hunger, and where millions are living at low physical energy because of insufficient nourishment. There are 500,000,000 people of our generation who have *never* had enough to eat, and who *never will* have enough.

This problem of hunger is doubtless one explanation for the willingness of people in many lands to listen to the false promises of Russian communism. In a recent address Dr. Karl T. Compton described the dangers ahead in these words:

> Certain to be critical sooner or later is the problem of over-population in a world of limited and diminishing natural resources. The conquest of disease, the elimination of famine, the hoped-for abolition of war, all result in increasing the population and the demands for production of food and goods. Population increase may have forced on our citizen of 2002 the beginning of some terrific social upheavals.

Many agencies are aware of the problem and are at work on the answer. The World Health Organization, the Food and Agricultural Organization of the United Nations, and the Point Four Program of the United States Government are pushing plans for the wise expenditure of public funds aimed at producing more food for the people in the world's hunger areas.

Chemists are researching deeply into the matter of producing carbohydrates and proteins from nonplant sources (as they have already produced synthetic fats in oleomargarine). At the same time, food companies are devising cheaper and more effective methods of mass production and distribution of standard foods.

Certain American foundations—notably the Rockefeller and the Ford Foundations—are sending scientists, emissaries, and organizers into far lands to teach, and to help, national leaders to produce more food for their people. The Christian churches of America are sending agricultural missionaries to these same lands—as some have been doing for many years. Scientific cocieties and institutions are searching out new mass resources of protein food, both on land and in the sea.

Among the latter is the Woods Hole Oceanographic Institution, at Woods Hole, Massachusetts, which was established twenty-two years ago by private philanthropy—the Rockefeller and Carnegie Foundations. After twenty years of painstaking research in the mysteries of the deep, today's scientists are beginning to know that there exists in the oceans of the world an untold wealth of protein foods which could be made available. The oceans cover 70 per cent of the globe, but now provide only 1 per cent of the human diet.

One of the promising leads in the development of these vast potential food resources is now coming from some of the scientists at Woods Hole. They are studying the nature of the ocean— its chemistry, physiography, and currents, and its many other characteristics in relation to the lives of its myriad inhabitants. And they are devising methods of education by which hungry people, with no knowledge of the sea, may eventually learn how to feed themselves from its bounty. From this private, voluntary scientific institution—operated without profit and outside governmental initiative—may come a program which will help forestall the social upheavals which Dr. Compton envisions as otherwise threatening mankind fifty years hence.

Pioneering in Community Health of the Future

"The Jungles of the City Slum." Early this year a round-table discussion by men distinguished in community welfare and health was sponsored by the Grant Foundation of New York—itself a private philanthropic organization created and endowed by the founder of the W. T. Grant chain of stores.

This foundation is taking a special interest in the field of social welfare. Under a financial subvention provided, experts in health and welfare, both governmental and private, were asked to consider what responsibility and opportunity private philanthropy has for improving community health in the future.

Brief excerpts from the opinions expressed by these experts may be of interest to the reader as we consider the challenging possibilities for creating a better world in the coming generation, and philanthropy's role in that creation. The theme of the round-table discussion was thus stated:

Can free philanthropic enterprise now influence significantly the course of modern health and welfare, as it did so notably during the early decades of this century?

Said Bradley Buell, executive director of Community Research Associates: "What is needed is the free investment of relatively small amounts of money at strategic spots in a manner that will result in the re-focussing, improvement and better co-ordination of the services that we now have. . . ."

Said Roscoe P. Kandle, field director of the American Public Health Association: "Wise philanthropy is essential if we are to make progress through the difficult problems which lie ahead. . . ."

Commented Dr. C.-E. A. Winslow, professor of public health, emeritus, Yale University: "Our speakers have answered the question of the evening with a more-or-less emphatic *Yes*. . . . The opportunities are almost limitless. The jungles of the Amazon are no more real than the jungles of the city slum and the rural tenement. . . ."

JUVENILE DELINQUENCY AND YOUTHFUL CRIME

If we wish one more indication of the urgent demands daily confronting all our social services, we need only to read the daily papers. A good example was a story in *The New York Times* of July 22, 1952, headlined "Delinquency Curb Held to Be Urgent—1,000,000 Young Wrongdoers in U.S. Now Seen Rising 50% Within Ten Years." The story seems to indicate that no matter how many agencies are at work, the problem is not being solved, and further urgent appeals for active help need to be made. The situation is stated strongly in the first paragraph:

Placing the problem of the country's juvenile delinquents squarely on the shrugging shoulders of an apathetic public and on inadequate public and private *child service agencies,* the Children's Bureau of the Federal Security Agency rallied representatives of *thirty national organizations* yesterday to discuss a national program to combat the condition. [The Italics are mine.]

Here, indeed, is a challenge to the combined religious, educational, and civic strength of America. The policemen, of course, backed by governmental finances and authority, must try to check crime on the spot where it is committed, and the courts must punish it. That is a duty of the tax-supported agencies of society. But policing alone will never deter juvenile delinquents. The chief deterrent must be in the hearts and characters of individuals, so that they will not *want* to attempt violations of law and decency. That is the duty and the opportunity of our homes, our schools and our churches, Protestant and Catholic and Jewish youth societies, Boy Scouts and Girl Scouts, settlement houses, and the thousands of other character-building agencies and societies. These are the personal forces rooted in the voluntary efforts of communities and groups and individuals all across the land. Here is, perhaps, the greatest opportunity and challenge to voluntary pioneering in our generation.

WORLD PEACE, MASS MARKETS, AND WORLD PROSPERITY

Look at one more problem—world peace and prosperity. Few thoughtful persons would doubt that if the free nations of the Western World would reduce their barriers to economic, financial, social, and political co-operation, a vast mass market and united strength would be created that would raise the level of living of all their people, and bring peace and hope to the whole world.

How may this be accomplished? It has been the hope and dream of men of vision for generations—of Grotius, Benjamin Franklin, Victor Hugo, Woodrow Wilson. But diplomats and governments have thus far been powerless to break the chains of ancient jealousies in order to set free this ideal. In our own generation two colossal wars have destroyed much of the wealth and power of the strongest nations. Governments have lost trillions of their capital and millions of their people as a penalty for not solving this eternal human problem.

Private citizens must help find the solution, as they are trying to do in many ways and in many nations.

Take *Europe*: In 1948 a group of private citizens, disappointed as they were in the postwar failures of their governments to create effective new patterns for European unity, convened at The Hague, calling themselves the Congress of Europe. Among the leaders were the Honorable Winston Churchill and Anthony Eden of England, Paul Reynaud of France, and Paul Van Zeeland of Belgium—all then out of public office. Eight hundred delegates responded to the invitation. All came as private citizens—none representing his government. In fact, among the delegates were twenty-six M.P.'s from England, who attended in spite of the complete opposition of the British Labour Government then in power.

These eight hundred leaders created the European Movement, which in recent years has been vigorously leading Western Europe toward greater unity. As an outgrowth of this voluntary activity by private citizens, there now begin to emerge—faintly but perceptibly—the outlines of the United States of Europe which is to be. The European Consultative Assembly, the Schuman Plan, the European Defense Community, and the other present cooperative movements in Europe are related to this symbol of united effort. Some day, if another terrible war does not intervene, the old barriers in Europe may come down and industry there may have a mass market—with the united strength, mutual aid, and general prosperity which will come in its wake.

In our own country, in 1949, a significant resolution was laid before the Senate. Introduced by Senator Estes Kefauver and supported by more than a score of other senators, the resolution, if passed, would request the President of the United States to call a convention of the Atlantic Treaty nations, with the objective of exploring the steps that could be taken to increase the co-operation—economic, political, industrial, financial, cultural —between the free nations of the Atlantic Community.

A committee consisting of ex-Supreme Court Justice Owen J.

Roberts, ex-Undersecretary of State Will L. Clayton, and Hugh Moore, a prominent manufacturer, visited the Secretary of State and asked him to give his support to this resolution. The Secretary declined on the grounds that to do so would put the United States in the position of advocating the measures which might be recommended—the government having no sanction for taking such an official position. He said, in effect: *"Why do you not, as private citizens, call such a convention, and thus point the way for future governmental action?"*

It is likely that just that will be done by a group of private citizens, now forming. If so, it will be one more instance of private philanthropy serving the public good with its own money and zeal, its own faith and vision—unselfishly pioneering an advance which may help to bring peace and well-being to a sick and war-frightened world.

CHAPTER XVIII

Today's Insistent Question—Voluntary or Compulsory?

THIS is a question which is rapidly shaping into one of the basic issues of our generation. Highlighted by the omnipresent impasse between East and West—between the totalitarian and the free nations—it is gradually beginning to emerge as an issue that will demand an answer in every area of personal and national life.

During the twenty-year period from 1933 to 1953, the Federal Government boldly took over responsibility for a great many programs of social betterment that had previously been assumed by voluntary philanthropy, or had been the responsibility of local government. Congress levied new federal taxes which increased in that period from seven to more than sixty-five billion dollars a year—of which several billions was for the financing of newly assumed social responsibilities. We began to be known as a "welfare state." In addition, Washington proposed to take over other large responsibilities in the fields of education and health; the majority of these plans have not been consummated.

The national election of 1952 had some clear-cut issues, well defined for the voters. Underneath these specific issues, in my opinion, ran a strong current of concern by the American people over the further development of a too centralized, "socializing" government at Washington. As I have suggested above, this may not have been a decisive issue in the 1952 national elections, but the more serious element of the electorate, who understand and appreciate the reasons for American strength and freedom, seemed to sense the recent trend away from personal and local responsibility to centralized authority, and to be deeply concerned over where it was leading.

Few would deny the responsibility of government at the federal, state, or local level to protect the welfare of the people. On the other hand, many have seen the dangers of a highly centralized government which seems to lift from the consciences and the minds of local citizens their own responsibilities for the well-being of themselves and their neighbors. In this chapter I should like to present some ideas and evidence on the importance of the voluntary element—as opposed to the compulsory—in its bearing on American freedom and American well-being.

THE POWER OF INITIATIVE

Several years ago I had an experience which gave me a healthy respect for the American plan of diffused responsibility and for the capabilities of American citizens to use their own initiative. As Lincoln said, "Throw the people on their own resources and then this Republic—the last possible hope of earth—will not perish out of the world."

A few months before our entry into World War II the Federal Government asked the various states to create state councils of defense for the purpose of mobilizing the power of the civilian population in the event of actual war. The legislature of Pennsylvania passed an act creating the Pennsylvania State Council of Defense, with the governor—the Honorable Arthur H. James—as chairman, and a dozen other state officials and private citizens as members. I was asked to serve as executive director of the Council, with my office at the state capitol. Marts and Lundy, Inc., and Bucknell University—my two employers—gave me leaves of absence.

The Honorable Fiorello H. La Guardia was then at Washington as head of the National Office of Civilian Defense. As we were trying to get the defense program organized in Pennsylvania, telegrams and letters began to pour into various parts of the state, instructing cities and communities as to various actions which Washington desired from them and requesting that reports of progress be sent to Washington. It was most confusing. The result was that the people throughout Pennsylvania tended more and more to sit back and wait for Washington to do something for them.

One day I gathered up a set of telegrams that Mr. La Guardia had sent to our mayors and went to Washington to see him. Showing him these telegrams, I explained the confusion that was resulting because Washington was not making use of the state office in its efforts to rally the people.

I told Mr. La Guardia that the Pennsylvania State Council had ample legal authority and ample administrative funds to do a thorough job of organizing civilian defense throughout the whole state, and that all we would need from his office would be technical information regarding the patterns of civilian defense desired throughout the nation and any other helps or aids that the national office could give the state office. I asked him how in the world his office in Washington could effectively make direct contact with the thousands of cities, counties, and communities throughout the nation except through the state councils. I pledged that the Harrisburg office would take all that detail for the State of Pennsylvania off his hands, and transfer the responsibility for action to local citizens in their own communities.

The "Little Flower" summoned his associates, held out the telegrams, and asked plaintively, "Did I send these?" When assured that he had, he immediately issued instructions that no more orders should go from Washington to any cities, communities, or counties of Pennsylvania, but that all instructions thereafter should go to the State Council of Defense at Harrisburg.

We promptly made contacts with the commissioners of each county, with the mayor of each city, and—through proper channels—with the governing commissioners of each town and village. Within four months there was a Council of Defense in each of the sixty-seven counties, in each of the cities, and in hundreds of towns and villages. Thousands of the best men and women of the state not subject to military service gave prompt and enthusiastic leadership, as volunteers in their local communities, to every aspect of the community defense program—air-raid wardens, auxiliary police, rescue squads, American Red Cross first-aid training, victory gardens, county and local rationing boards, and so on. Within a few months 1,250,000 citizens—better than one out of ten—were busily at work in their own communities, under their own leadership on a voluntary, noncompensated basis, carrying out the entire National Civilian Defense Program.

Governor James then invited the "Little Flower" to come to Pennsylvania to inspect the civilian defense forces. Mayor La Guardia was good enough to say that, under our system of decentralizing responsibility back to the local communities where the citizens were eager to take full initiative, the Commonwealth of Pennsylvania was one of the two best organized states in the Union. The confusion and delay engendered by unwise centralized administration from Washington turned into strength and self-sufficiency under the system of voluntary community responsibility which is at the very heart of our American Democracy.

As I understand the political philosophy of Thomas Jefferson, who had so great a share in creating our system of government and society, it could be summed up in the word "diffusion"— diffusion of authority and of responsibility. Jefferson and most of his colleagues in the drafting of the Constitution dreaded and feared a powerful centralized government. They did all they could to distribute responsibility—even to the tiniest village and to the individual citizen. They provided relatively small tax revenue for the National Government, and as little specific administrative authority as possible. As Jefferson declared: "That country is governed best which is governed least."

Has not diffusion of responsibility been one of the secrets of our great democratic strength? It has laid upon small local governments—close to their citizens—and upon voluntary philanthropic agencies a great share of the load of community welfare. And the private citizen of America has proved himself capable of carrying that load. America's power has thus become the aggregate power of millions of unseen people, rather than the spectacular power of a "chief of state." This was always so until economic disaster struck us in the early 1930's, with the accumulated aftermath of a World War and a resulting world depression.

THE COMING OF NEW IDEAS

While we were struggling twenty years ago with these desperate conditions and seeking the answers to problems that seemed not to yield promptly to traditional treatment, new ideas from across the Atlantic were being carefully cultivated here by the brain-trusters of a young generation, who had been intrigued by a vision of the oncoming social revolution.

Perhaps these were the revolutionary ideas that President Woodrow Wilson foresaw in 1919, when he said:

Money coming from nobody knows where is deposited, by the millions, in capitals like Stockholm, to be used for the propaganda of disorder and discontent and dissolution throughout the world, and men look you calmly in the face in America and say they are for that sort of revolution—when that sort of revolution means government by terror, government by force, not government by vote.

It is the negation of everything that is American; but it is spreading, and so long as disorder continues, so long as the world is kept waiting for the answer to the question—What kind of peace are we going to have and what kind of guarantees are there to be behind that peace?—that poison will steadily spread more and more rapidly, spread until it may be that even this beloved land of ours will be distracted and distorted by it.

We began to hear Keynesian theories of government spending and pump-priming. We began to hear of social security, and parity and beneficent deficits and unbalanced budgets, and sit-down strikes and thirty-five-hour work weeks, and other concepts entirely contrary to older American convictions about thrift, economy, balanced budgets, hard work, provision for the rainy day, and youthful ambition and struggle.

We even began to hear words to the effect that man's misfortunes are society's blame—some even proclaimed that the youth who seeks only for a chance to show what he is worth is a bit of a sap in a world that owes him a living.

Many of the older traditional virtues in American life were ridiculed and weakened by this new "wave of the future" that swept across our country during the thirties and the forties. Fortunately, private philanthropy—while one of the oldest virtues in American life—withstood these onslaughts more sturdily than did some other traditional virtues. It proved too firmly rooted in American experience to give way to the new enthusiasm for statism and socialism. But, while it has stood its ground and increased the extent of its operations in American life, its *relative* place has of course decreased as governmental spending for social services has pyramided. The danger in American life in our generation is not that private philanthropy will wither and die, but that centralized government may so strengthen itself and reach so deeply into the life of the local community that eventually the private citizen will feel little responsibility for what happens in his own neighborhood.

Two recent statements by eminent Americans sum up well the conflict of opinions on this vital and basic issue. Said Charles P. Taft of Cincinnati, son of the late President Taft and recently president of the Federal Council of Churches:

> The State for us is no divine entity to be obeyed of itself. It is a tool for the people's progress. . . . This elimination of the absolute State is part of our common Western inheritance, with Europe, from the Greeks and the Jews.

And, from the opposing viewpoint, I quote a sentence from a book by one considered a leading educator of our time:

> Each of us, in a well-organized society, yields to the State all that he is, all that he has, and in doing so each of us becomes a free person.

David Lawrence, in *U. S. News and World Report*, recently noted the change in attitude toward the state that has taken place in America during the present century, in these words:

> Fifty years ago a "liberal" was a person who didn't want the Constitution narrowly construed so that individual rights would be curtailed. Today a "liberal" is one who wants the Constitution to authorize the Federal Government to control, through the State, the life of the individual.

Pope Pius XII, in his 1953 message to the world, warned against this ominous trend away from freedom. He said:

> In some countries the modern State is becoming a gigantic administrative machine. It extends its influence over almost every phase of life. It would bring under its administration the entire gamut of political, economic, social and intellectual life from birth to death.

Here may be recognized the origin and sum of that phenomenon which is submerging modern man under its tide of anguish: his depersonalization. . . .

No wonder then, if in this impersonal atmosphere, which tends to penetrate and pervade all human life, respect for the common good becomes dormant in the conscience of individuals, and the State loses more and more its primary character of a community of morally responsible citizens.

PHILANTHROPY AND INDIVIDUAL FREEDOM

In this conflict of ideas, voluntary philanthropy is part and parcel of the concept of diffusion of government, of the responsibility of free men and women.

There are at least three distinctive strands of American democracy which are interwoven inextricably in the fabric of our society: *localized government,* by which the citizens of even the smallest communities administer the laws that regulate them; *free enterprise* in business, which enables our people to devote their brains and energies to the creation and distribution of new resources; and *voluntary philanthropy,* through which devoted men and women in each generation give time, money, and talent to the spiritual services of our nation without let or hindrance from politicians.

We frequently think of our freedom as the freedom to vote and to elect our public officials. But this is but the beginning. Not the least of our freedoms is freedom to give.

The Honorable Newton D. Baker, Secretary of War during World War I, once said:

The Government is now committed to the task of making life possible. We private individuals must unite to make it worthwhile.

President Theodore Roosevelt—always a champion of self-reliance and individual initiative—recognized the voluntary element as one of the prized values of American life. Repeatedly, he voiced the conviction that "every man and woman in the land ought to prize above almost every other quality the capacity for self-help."

President Grover Cleveland thus summed it up in his own terse manner:

It is the duty of every citizen to support his government; it is not the obligation of the government to support the citizens.

Governor Thomas E. Dewey of New York said in 1953:

Something is wrong, and unless we do something about it the dead hand of government will take over a field which requires the imagination and genius of free men.

John Foster Dulles, Secretary of State, said in December, 1952, in an address before the National Council of Churches:

Perhaps the best thing our government can do toward ending world conditions of peril and insecurity would be to encourage and make place for the individual and group effort which are the most precious jewels of freedom.

Nothing has been more disastrous to the cause of freedom than our growing assumption that nothing happens unless government does it. The basic solution of today's problems rests with free individuals and their private institutions.

It is different when individuals and private groups freely give of their own, out of a sense of compassion, particularly if they express that compassion in intelligent and constructive ways. . . .

Speaking on the same occasion about government and unofficial aid given abroad, he said:

The $40,000,000,000 our government has dispensed abroad since the end of World War II has failed to make the friends which might have been made had greater effort at smaller expense been made by semi-private and unofficial American agencies and organizations. Good relations between governments do not necessarily imply good relations between peoples. But good relations between peoples can compel good relations between governments.

Governor Adlai Stevenson recognized the peculiar value of the voluntary element in a brief radio address he made on November 11, 1952, in launching the 1953 Crusade for Freedom—that endeavor of American citizens to break through the Iron Curtain with a message of hope to the freedom-loving peoples behind that tragic barrier.

In praising the private and voluntary character of the Crusade, he said:

There is a spontaneity and freshness about Radio Free Europe and Radio Free Asia which no *official* information agency can ever have. Freedom's most appealing voice is that from man to man.

Even more pointed are the following words spoken by President Eisenhower, in the course of informal remarks made on March 14, 1953, to the American Medical Association House of Delegates meeting in Washington:

I don't like the word "compulsory." I am against the word "socialized."

Everything about such words seems to me to be a step toward the thing that we are spending so many billions to prevent; that is, the overwhelming of this country by any force, power, or idea that leads us to forsake our traditional system of free enterprise.

THE PRESERVATION OF FREEDOM

There will always be more to be done than all our forces— private and public—can ever do. It is not just a question of "either-or," voluntary or compulsory. It is a question of how a given thing can best be done, if it can and should be done, and by whom. It is not always easy to find the right dividing line. And the basic question that must always be in our thoughts is this: How can we cure an evil or injustice without lessening our diffused freedom and strength?

If human beings are to be transformed we know that it takes time, skill, and patience. Here, what has been called "totalitarian democracy" differs sharply from the American ideal of diffused responsibility and private philanthropy. In reviewing J. L. Talmon's recent book, *The Rise of Totalitarian Democracy*, in *The New York Times*, Crane Brinton writes:

What drove Rousseau in theory—and his followers, Robespierre and Babeuf, in practice—to sacrifice individual liberty and variety for authority and uniformity, is to him their impatient idealism, their messianic drive to make human beings into what they felt human beings should be.

They were *idealists in a hurry*—in so much of a hurry that in their rush they lost the better part of their ideals.

More and more I have come to feel that if ever there should arise in America a lazy or thoughtless generation which would be content to allow a powerful government, rich with fabulous tax levies, to lift the responsibilities of community betterment from the shoulders of local citizens, it is likely future historians would record that that generation marked the beginning of the decline of the power and usefulness of this nation.

Dr. Harry Emerson Fosdick, with his usual eloquence, clearly contrasted the compulsory and voluntary elements in American life in the sermon which he delivered a few years ago at the funeral of Sidney R. Kent, one of the most respected motion picture executives. He found in the life and action of the man "the innermost principle which unites freedom in art and freedom in politics." He continued:

Our fathers at their best had a powerful voluntary life. In this country they widened for us, as never had been done before in history, the realm of self-directed, self-controlled, self-dedicated living. They trusted us to go on with that. But that order of life is not merely a political system, self-perpetuating. The maintenance of that order of life depends upon the maintenance of the free and voluntary spirit in the people, creating uncoerced character, conduct and public spirit. Democracy depends upon volunteers.

Whenever coercion increases, as it does today, that means that voluntariness has failed. Whenever in any realm the government cannot get enough volunteers, it necessarily turns to compulsion. Here is a truth, without seeing which I think we cannot understand the major problems of our social life today. When coercion increases and multiplies its impositions, that is because the voluntary—that is to say, the free spiritual—life has failed.

For life is divided into two parts: the compulsory and the voluntary. They are like the sea and the land. They share the earth between them.

The more there is of one—the less there is of the other. We therefore have our choice: we can develop in ourselves and in our nation a strong and fruitful spiritual life that creates uncompelled character and public spirit; or, if we fail in that, coercion will come flooding in like an encroaching sea. That is the inexorable alternative.

CHAPTER XIX

Voluntary Philanthropy Beckons America Forward

> O beautiful for patriot dream
> That sees beyond the years,
> Thine alabaster cities gleam,
> Undimmed by human tears!
> America! America!
> God shed His grace on thee,
> And crown thy good with brotherhood
> From sea to shining sea.
> —KATHARINE LEE BATES

I SHOULD now like to ask the reader's forbearance while I do a little adding up, in the hope that it may shed light on the role that philanthropy is capable of playing in the unpredictable future where America must lead the way.

Briefly, we have seen that the love of mankind is a deep, permanent instinct. Perhaps it is the instinct that most clearly sets man apart from the animals—that makes a soul human. From earliest times it has been related to religion—in at least a vague feeling that God was good and wanted men to be helpful to each other.

The historic development of the Judaeo-Christian religion, as revealed in the Old and New Testaments, clarified these concepts. Philanthropy received a perfect charter in Jesus' own summary of His message:

Thou shalt love the Lord thy God with all thy heart and with all thy soul and with all thy mind; and *thy neighbor as thy self.*

And in the parable of the good Samaritan—a representative of an alien, despised group—He answered the question "Who is my neighbor?" and showed how human sympathy overleaps all bounds.

As the centuries passed, the dynamic in the Christian gospel—"the good seed"—bore many fruits. As Europe came out of the Dark Ages, Church-inspired educational and humanitarian institutions multiplied, grew strong, and stamped their impress indelibly upon Western civilization.

Finally, with the seventeenth-century founding of substantial American colonies, these institutions proliferated in a big new country, where there was room for growth in a climate of freedom. Here voluntary activities came to full stature.

Europe marveled. The penetrating French observer de Tocqueville—quoted on an opening page—could not get over his amazement at the way Americans in their local communities took complete initiative in creating whatever nongovernmental agencies they felt would be for the general good.

PHILANTHROPY IN AMERICA TODAY

Several chapters were devoted to tracing how various types of philanthropic activity developed: the influence of organized churches, the strong personal motives that have entered in, the peculiar genius of Americans for sustained cooperation, and also to the quiet and persistent education of public awareness that has led government to assume many activities now considered a public responsibility.

Lastly, we presented evidence to show that in spite of vastly extended governmental participation in these fields, *voluntary philanthropy continues to grow.*

No thoughtful person minimizes the present world-wide struggle between the compulsory and the voluntary—between totalitarian force and individual aspirations for freedom. In one form or another, this struggle colors every discussion of public policy and every problem of statecraft.

A keen analysis of the oft-noted American gift for individual action was recently made by Elliott E. Cohen in *Commentary,* a monthly magazine he edits for the American Jewish Committee. These words seem to me significant:

. . . . The individual (in the United States), in his struggle against the elephantiasis of modern institutions, is not alone, and is not powerless. Beyond and above . . . major ethnic and religious groupings there is the host of cellular structures which de Tocqueville noted so many years ago—the bewildering proliferation of private citizens' groups, formed by free association, in which Americans almost instinctively seem to join to carry out the most diverse aims and purposes, from the highest to the most trivial: fraternal orders, educational, health and social-welfare associations, neighborhood and regional organizations, associations for the slaughter of wild life and for the preservation of wild life, together with all varieties of associations for the protection of economic, financial, class, and occupational interests. . . .

Indeed, the initiative these groups display, the sheer amount of work they voluntarily carry through, may well be the single most extraordinary phenomenon in the United States. Sometimes one feels these are not only a supporting, supplementary force, but the very social fabric itself. . . .

In this book we have, of course, been particularly concerned with those voluntary activities directly related to philanthropic projects; but on every hand there is a growing feeling that "freedom is indivisible"—that our various freedoms will stand or fall together. It is because I have so often seen the philanthropic impulse reveal itself as one of the most vitalizing forms of freedom that I believe it is making a unique contribution to America's basic creed and working platform.

AN AMERICAN PLATFORM

The chief planks in that platform all seem related to *freedom*, and many of them—in one way or another—to philanthropy. Let me name some, as I see them:

1. Christian faith and ideals, planted by the Pilgrims and fully recognized by the Founding Fathers. Thus our country was created as a Christian nation, conceived in the spirit of the golden rule. A striking bit of current evidence is the fact that *The Indianapolis Star* recently changed its masthead motto from "Fair and First" to "Where the Spirit of the Lord is, There is

Liberty." In his editorial announcement Eugene Pulliam, the publisher, squarely commented:

> It is the Christian doctrine of all Christian churches that there can be no liberty without God. No nation of free men has ever existed for long unless the idea of God existed, and lived in the hearts of its citizens.

2. Freedom of worship—and *for* worship—with full respect for every man's honest religious faith. There seems to be a growing conviction that we should allow no obstacles to be placed in the way of desired religious education.

3. Freedom of expression and discussion in pursuit of truth. And the spirit of the old town meeting lives on in the feeling of community responsibility and in the desire for local self-government.

4. Freedom of action and of status, which received such a boost from the pioneering required in a new country, is one of the strongest features of our civilization.

5. Freedom of initiative and enterprise, which sets no artificial bounds to what a man can do, what he can save, and what he can build—for himself and for the future.

6. Freedom of association, groups of all kinds, for the pursuit of common interests and worthy ends. This implies full freedom of choice in the giving of one's time and money, after his legal duties have been met.

7. In pursuit of these ends, freedom of the individual citizen from tyranny by government. This means a complete renunciation of totalitarian statism.

Thus, in many directions, the traditional American creed supports—and in turn is supported by—the spirit of voluntary philanthropy. This spontaneous, uncoerced banding together of free men to further their mutual well-being is close to the heart of the American Way.

There are doubtless still some people who think of philanthropic activity as a frill, a nonessential. It is something much deeper, more powerful, than that. It has proved itself to be the yeast of civilization—"the leaven that leaveneth the whole lump."

If this be true—and who would controvert it?—should not those who solicit their fellow men for funds for philanthropic agencies do so with pride in a high calling? And should not those who give do so with a sense of the honor in participating in one of the oldest and noblest traditions of American freedom?

WHAT OF THE FUTURE ROLE?

Philanthropy's greatest role now beckons, for its stage is the world. It is bound to play its part in America's crusade in which, as President Eisenhower said in his challenging inaugural address: "Freedom is pitted against slavery; light against the darkness. The faith we hold belongs not to us alone but to the free of all the world. . . . Whatever America hopes to bring to pass in the world must first come to pass in the heart of America."

Both in personal and national life new currents are flowing. Americans have long given the "go-getter" his full due. He has often been a true builder of our civilization, full of the aggressiveness so often needed in a new country. We are now increasingly appreciative of the "go-giver" as often a still better prophet, a better pioneer, a better builder. I propose that we recognize the modern go-giver for all that he has meant to America—honor him and join him. There is still much to be done.

Bishop Fulton J. Sheen wrote in a recent article:

The vast majority of the people in Western civilization are engaged in the task of getting. Strange as it may seem, the Christian ethic is founded on the opposite principle—that *it is more blessed to give than to receive.*

Thus, philanthropy is in many cases simply applied Christianity. It is an endless extension of the program of One who "went about doing good," and who promised His followers: "Greater things than these shall ye do." And the idea of conscientious stewardship—with the moral obligation to be frugal, watchful, far-sighted—is also made emphatic in some of Jesus' most picturesque parables. This is another important plank in modern philanthropy. In fact, a catalogue of leading Christian virtues and attitudes comes close to describing the perfect philanthropist. He is a man of peace, of good will, of mercy, of humility, of sympathy, of patience, of generosity, of understanding. The classic description of "charity"—or love—in the 13th Chapter of 1st Corinthians strikes the perfect note. And as James Russell Lowell puts it in *The Vision of Sir Launfal:*

> Who giveth himself with his gift feeds three:
> Himself, his hungering neighbor, and Me.

Ours is a noble way in which to build a just and free civilization—the way which has been evolved over the generations in America. Out of its heart, and within its means and knowledge, each generation freely creates and maintains its agencies to right injustices, to heal the sick, to educate and inspire the young, to assuage the sorrow of the old and the lonely, to make life more kindly and better for all. We believe this to be true democracy in action. It is a program in which every man and woman may or may not take part, as he or she may choose or be able. The rewards to those who do take part are inspiring, and rich in the coin of satisfaction.

The other way—preferred by present-day followers of Marx, Lenin, and Stalin—discards and belittles the whole concept of free peoples improving their social conditions by spontaneous voluntary efforts. Their method is that of compulsion by a tyrannical central government toward the falsely professed goal of human justice and equality. To cause the masses of the people to conform to the plans of the few at the top, this compulsion uses such terrible weapons as slave camps, imprisonment, and the "purge." Even though in the beginning their plans and hopes might conceivably have been aimed at a Utopia of freedom and justice, the very methods which they have used have created more human misery and suffering amongst the masses than this world has experienced since the dark ages.

A WORLD ROLE BECKONS

A long generation ago—before World War I—there was much serious talk of needing "a moral equivalent for war." This phrase, coined by William James, seemed then to catch the imagination. It assumed that wars had ended. Thoughtful men realized that most human beings needed a supreme challenge—needed to face something difficult that had to be done, some cause that had to be won—if their deepest and most unselfish powers were to be developed to the utmost.

Looking back into our early American history, it is clear that such challenges constantly faced our pioneering predecessors. They formed the daily environment in which these men, some of whose stories we have told, grew strong. It was their struggles against odds, the stark necessity of doing much with little, that called out their creative powers, that developed their initiative and courage. Common problems and common dangers developed their co-operation.

Today, we have had only too much experience with war itself. The world has never devised another such expensive way to develop character. When we used to talk of seeking a "moral equivalent for war," we were paying armed conflict far too high a compliment. For everyone whose soul is ennobled by the stern facing of service and sacrifice, a thousand find their souls seared by tragic loss and disillusionment. How many are there whose bodies are bent and broken by the physical blows of armed strife? How many communities and lands have been desolated and bankrupted by the ghastly destruction of material wealth and spiritual hope alike?

On the other hand, consider how the efforts to create, to build helpful services, to pioneer humanitarian advances, have ennobled men, have healed bodies, have brought food to growing minds, skill to unskilled hands, hope to discouraged souls. This is the endless, world-wide battle that every true lover of mankind is waging. Some of the leaders and some of the victories in the age-long warfare we have tried to sketch.

And may there not be deep meaning in the fact that America—a land of destiny, put here to accomplish something for the good of all mankind, to share its dream with all nations—is the land where voluntary philanthropy, the unselfish will to better man's lot, has come into fullest flower and fruit? That flower—the American dream—has brought forth, as its fruit, the American Way.

May not the spirit of philanthropy, through us, now continue to be called upon to play a leading role in building a world civilization in which all men of good will may rejoice?

Index

Set in Linotype Baskerville
Format by Edwin H. Kaplin
Manufactured by The Haddon Craftsmen, Inc.
Published by HARPER & BROTHERS, *New York*